knuckle sandwich

I0470599

anji marth

knuckle sandwich

by Anji Marth

copyright 2002-2013

First edition, 9-23-2013

ISBN-10:
1492805386
ISBN 13:
978-1492805380

For Hawkins.

With thanks to the HP tribe.

CONTENTS

MADNESS	9
TATTOO TALES	23
TATTOOING	33
ARTS	49
INTERNETS	65
WILD THEORIES	77
MOTIVATION	99
COMPLAINTS	111
TALES	127
TRUE CRIMES	151
AFTERWORD	163
FINAL NOTES	166

Anji Marth: Dark art maker. Child-Pie maker.

Master of the arabesque and macabre. Dog treat

slinger. Hibernator.

Don't need money,don't need fame,don't need a

credit card because we take fucking cash only!

Probably too late. Been working

everywhere since I quit the shop. You know how it

goes.

~N. Porter, 2013

This book was written over the course of the last ten years, about half of it came from writings I did online. Some of it is from private journals and correspondence, and some is new for this publication. I hope you enjoy reading it, even though I only enjoyed writing some of it. I've tried to include even the most unfounded rants, as well as solid information, and some fiction.

I leave it to you to decide which category each bit fits.

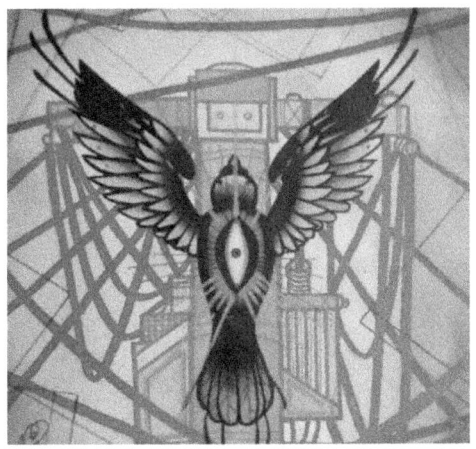

~ Anji Marth, September, 2013

Spokane, Washington

MADNESS

On suicide.

In 2003, on the 4th of July, I tried to kill myself.
from that time:

"I feel pain, and I don't know where to put it or what to do. I am also SO FUCKING ANGRY that I wanna blow up, tear up, the world sometimes. I am striving not to take that out on the people around me. I am striving for "alone time". I am striving for...clarity. I cannot make up my mind about anything. Everything I could do now that is good, feels like my second choice in direction, and not a close second either, but a booby prize. And I don't know if I can do all the things the world wants me to do and that I'm supposed to do, because I feel utterly exhausted even thinking about the smallest thing."

Mopery! (I know mopery actually means something else.) I was utterly destroyed at the time. I had been in my worst, lowest kind of depression for months, and then began a long protracted breakup as well, that weekend.

It was one of the lowest times of my entire life. I lived through it, and it's a little fresh today, so I won't go into too much detail right now. But I will say that I have not tried again, my life has changed for the better, and my ability to weather down times has grown- and that I am glad I survived, and am here.

I wasn't selfish- I was in pain. I wasn't a coward- I was at the end of my rope. I know that if you have never been that far down, inside, you don't understand that. I am glad that you don't because it really is bad. Suicide, for some people at some times, is like a dog chewing off a leg to escape a trap.

The amount of pain required for someone to seriously decide to die is immense. If you knew someone who was allergic to chlorine, and you lived in your pool, would you expect them to stand chest-deep in chlorinated water with you?

The reason crazy can be fatal is because the pain it causes is extreme and intense. There are no "life changes" or actions one can take to feel better or resolve it, it's a matter of brain chemistry. Some people find relief in medication, or even ECT (shock therapy) but there are in fact barriers in place to getting these treatments. Such as lack of funds, insurance, or simply the fear of being seen as weak- the stigma of being mentally ill is a big thing.

When you decide to commit suicide, you are not doing it as the easy way out. You're not thinking of how sad other people might get. It's purely a need to stop the pain, sometimes pain that is completely overwhelming.

I suffered for about a year before I attempted. I stayed alive, in the pain, because I was concerned about how it would affect the people I loved. I suffered for a year thinking only about everyone but myself.

I fully intended to die and was not only embarrassed as hell to find myself still alive afterward, but I was also in even more agony. It was bad.

I did of course survive, and because of that attempt was able to finally access treatment for my depression and psychosis that I was going through- but there are many people who don't survive the attempt. They are not selfish people. They are finally out of the pain they were experiencing.

It is painful to lose someone. It hurts. It's understandable to be angry, or to have harsh feelings about death of a loved one. But to consider suicide as a selfish act misses the point. It is the negation of self, the absolute negation of the self, that suicide is all about.

the darkness.

It is so hard to tell you.

It comes as a wave. It builds. It is slow, and heavy, and

at first it feels as if I can continue to stand in it, and resist the current.

When one's body is broken, it is visible. Others can see the broken parts sticking out, smell the rot, assess the damage and quantify the exact amount of sympathy, decide upon a course of action. The dark inside is different. The body shows it, yes, but not in ways that can be understood by anyone who has not been sucked under.

The darkness rises, and the current underneath will lift and grab. One's whole being, the air around, the muscles give way.

Just get up. Just shower and shave and do the dishes and feed the dog and wash the clothes and cook food and pay a bill and go to work and

None of these things are possible. When you're standing on the shore these are easy things, simple, small things. In the grip of the current the only fight is not to get sucked under completely, to keep the head above the surface enough to steal a breath.

And another, and another. Because you can't just stop breathing.

I know I should just talk directly about my own experience, here. I know I should be specific. But how can

I? How can I?

I have smelled my own stench when a week of the darkness has left me washed up on the shore. I've been catatonic- seen shapes in the shadows. I've felt pain in places where my body is not. And when the body is hurt, broken, or ill, the darkness knows, and rushes forward to seize its chance.

Being alone, in pain, and having the dark wash up on you is something you must, and most will, experience in life. You cannot understand it until it comes, and when you have been through it you will have changed. The darkness leaves a mark on you that can't be washed away by all the sunlight and blowing curtains and fresh water you can muster.

It passes, and it's gone. Once it's come and gone you know it can come again, though. And that haunted feeling will stay.

Good times are good times. And they are best because the darkness has been and gone. The shadows make all the light around them richer.

Pills.

In the morning, I take the top row of pills, all of them, everyday.

That's two 200mg seroquel, and two 40mg prozac capsules. And to the right, Chantix.

I take this as soon as I open my eyes. Sometimes (almost always) I stay in bed or maybe even go back to sleep for a bit; but it's the first thing I do in the morning.

At night, I take one of the leftmost pills on the bottom row- I alternate them. One is lunesta, one is ambien, one is temazepam. I take a different one each night so they all keep working. And, along with that, I take my second chantix.

I've had insomnia as long as I can remember. The last year or so with these medicines, I have been able to fall asleep far easier and more consistently than ever before. Not that I don't still sleep in, because I do. But at least I don't stay up all night then sleep an hour or two- or sleep ALL day everyday.

"I am crazy wild this minute"

Selections from the book "The Inner World of Mental Illness", published by Harper & Row in 1964. It's one of my favorite books, written by a variety of people in very different circumstances and with very different afflictions; all the stories have the same undertone of fear, grieving, and pragmatism.

I've read this book to shreds, literally.

Most of the chapters in it are excerpts from longer books written by the mentally ill, but some are merely short pieces, collected by doctors or nurses. I'll post more of these if enough of you want more of them.

The book includes a variety of mental illnesses, so if you'd like an excerpt dealing with some other disorder, let me know in the comments and I'll do my best.

This excerpt is from "I am crazy wild this minute", written by Lara Jefferson in the 40s. It was written on scrap paper and wrapping paper in a state hospital.

When her writing was discovered by staff, she was given a typewriter and encouraged to continue. Hospitals at that time were much more chaotic, and psychosis was not treated with as much compassion or medical understanding as it is today.

Had I been born in the age and time when the world dealt in a straightforward manner with misfits as could not meet the requirements of living, I would not have been much of a problem to my contemporaries. They would have said that I was "Possessed of the Devil" and promptly stoned me to death- or else disposed of me in some other equally effective manner.

"I know I cannot think straight- but the conclusions I

arrive at are very convincing to me and I still think the whole system is a regular Hades itself. ...

I cannot conduct myself as the rules set forth because something has broken loose within me and I am insane- and differ from these others to the extent that I still have sense enough to know it; which is a mark of spectacular intelligence- so they tell me.

Here I sit- mad as the hatter- with nothing to do but either become madder and madder- or else recover enough of my sanity to be allowed to go back to the life which drove me mad.

If that is not a vicious circle, I hope I never encounter one. But today the circle has stopped chasing itself long enough to drop me somewhere along the unmarked line between stark lunacy and harmless eccentricity. The latter is as near to normal as I ever hope to get. I am not relying on my opinion in that matter. The doctor was through just now...

For all I know of what he said, he might have been swearing at me in Yiddish. But I did get this much out of his very learned discourse- ...that unless I learn some new mental habits- and learn them in a hurry one of these days in the not far distant future I am going to find myself over on "Three Building"- and when you land in "Three Building" you have fallen to the very bottom, you are hopelessly and incurably insane.

Unless I learn to think differently, I shall shortly be incurably insane. There it is before me in words- small, black words, written with one hand and a stub of pencil- and on my ability to do what he admitted was one of the "impossibles" my fate is hanging."

She goes on to speak of how she was institutionalized:

"It did overtake me in my twenty-ninth year. It caught me and swept me...I can recall with humor the odd sensation that a crazy woman had moved into my body. A crazy woman who had no sense at all, and who refused to be governed by reason- who acknowledged no law higher than her own whim- and who had no fear of anything.

...To others, I was only a maniac, howling, but who, by some odd quirk of nature had the canny foresight to ask for a straight-jacket before madness claimed me.

I was locked away in a cell, stark madness my only companion. Had I been the sole inhabitant of some distant star, I could not have been more alone. It was not a brass lock which taught me what the nakedness and loneliness of living means."

And speaks at length about her treatments, the medicine and "cures" administered to her and others on the ward.

"I know now how rats and rabbits and guinea pigs feel

when they are vivisected. Vivisection is painful- and let those who think it isn't, get themselves pronounced insane...This is the Bug-house, the Bughouse- the Bug-house!... The place where Nuts are kept. Never mind our protests. All that is done for us is good for us. It is just our hard luck that we have no comprehension.

The nurses are feeding one of the patients now. She would not eat. Did not want to eat. But they are pouring the food down her anyway. They have a wooden peg in her mouth and are crouched behind a sheet held up like a shield, because the woman tries to spew each mouthful upon them...she is tied down in a straight-jacket and can do nothing but spit and curse and howl.

...She is mad with her impotence and helplessness so she hates the nurses with fury unbelievable."

She discusses the other patients, and the intensity of mental illness as well.

"We cannot cope with life as we find it, nor can we escape it or adjust ourselves to it. So we are given the power to create some sort of world we can deal with. The worlds created are as varied as there are minds to create them. Each one is strictly private and cannot be shared with another. It is much more real than reality.

For nothing that happens to a sane mortal in the common-place world of ordinary living, can approach the startling intensity of things going on in a delusion. There is a sharpness, a shrillness, a piercing intensity that thrusts itself through …and is ever so much more convincing than the blunt edge of reason, that even if the two are conflicting there is no choice between them. Reason is beaten, dismissed and defeated at the very outset, it cannot content with the saber edge of delusion.

Those who are tied down are howling and shrieking, and those who are loose are racing and charging about and adding wild gesticulations to their howls and shrieks. They all seem like bare trees in a forest through which the wind of their madness is sweeping; bowing them, bending them, breaking them."

and she speaks directly to future readers, too.

"Sometimes the break comes slowly, a pressure unmarked at the first, but slowly rising. A gnawing discontent; a childish fear that swings onward and outward in an ever widening orbit etching itself into the mysterious force called personality. Then Ruin follows. For Ruin it most surely is; as any know who have stood beside a fellow being strapped hand and foot to save himself and others from his fury. We call it Ruin; this collapse of faculties where reason is displaced by demoniac delusions; where staid and ordered thought gives way and the sense run riot. Ruin.

However, like all other happenings, the viewpoint

modifies the scene. I who stand on the other side of this phenomenon called madness, would like to stretch a hand across to those who may some day go through it. Or stand by someone they love and watch the barrier rising; see the gulf, more grim than death, across which there is no reaching. They learn what real loss is...

To those I would speak and say; "Remember, when a soul sails out on that unmarked sea they have gained release much greater than your loss- and more important... Salvation from a much greater pain than the stark pain of madness."

...Once the madness in me found a voice, there was no stopping it.

It is not imagination- it is something much stronger.

After my break and confinement, the answer came to me in a flash of brilliancy. I was a mental misfit. Like an alcoholic who knows he cannot take even one drink or a diabetic who must forever forego any sugar, I knew I must pass up all depressive thinking, and delusions. It would be impossible to swear off forever, but I could live here hour by hour. Day by day I sat here and wrote about it- for there was nothing else in all the world to do."

bullying and the crazies

Mental illness is often fatal.

I've been reading a ton about bullying against the young

gay community and while I understand the well-meant interest in homophobic bullying specifically I do think a serious problem is being glossed over.

See, loads of glbt youth are bullied. Most of them do not commit suicide. People arr involuntarily outed all the time, often in humiliating ways: most do not choose to die because of this.

It is when a kid who is glbt is also mentally ill that suicide comes up. Being that conservative factions have caused an atmosphere of fear among counselors and teachers, kids who are mentally ill and in need of encouragement and help are often AFRAID to ask for it because of their orientation. They aren't stupid. They know that any effort to help their depression or mental health issues will mean COMING OUT TO A SCHOOL OR MEDICAL AUTHORITY FIGURE who, most likely, will frown upon or judge them; at very least will not encourage them in optimism for their future.

In this way, gay kids are DENIED the basic counseling and mental health services they may need.

Untreated mental illness can be fatal.

Being gay, however, no matter the level of bullying, IS NOT THE CAUSE OF SUICIDE.

It is underlying depression or other real illness that causes some people to turn to suicide as a solution.

We need to make counselors and teachers aware that

students who need help MUST NOT BE JUDGED and their privacy during assessment MUST BE RESPECTED. The atmosphere of hate and prejudice which is at this time institutionalized in our school systems is to blame for these deaths-

Although bullying is a terrible thing, it alone doesn't kill. It's the combination of innate depression that is untreated, bullying from peers, and lack of caring, unbiased adult assistance that is deadly.

We need to make mental health services available and care for kids who need help, regardless their gender or orientation. Then things won't have to get better LATER ON. Things can be better NOW.

TATTOO TALES

the tribe.

When I started tattooing, anyone I saw with large, visible work was very nearly guaranteed to be someone who was in my tribe. I don't mean tribe in the sense that we shared every opinion, but that we shared the expectation of being considered somewhat beyond the margins of the common, outside the mainstream, someone who was not acceptable in mixed company. We were subversive. I could look at someone, see their work, and know they were on my side of that equation.

Because of this, I felt a connection to everyone I worked on. I could open up to them, exchange ideas and energy with them, and really bond. We both knew, after all, what it was like to be outcast, to be strange, to be the "Other".

That has changed. Now, at work, I block energy. I try to keep things light, and a bit distant. I only can connect like this after I have worked on someone a few times and gotten to know them. There are exceptions, of course. But the exceptions are indeed exceptional.

I don't think that my own approach to my work can change this. I can educate people about getting better tattoos, but the kind of life experience and wisdom that a tattoo used to signify is NOT something that can be bought, or sold.

You have to earn it in your own life, with your own bitter tears.

Nobody can give it to you in a few hours for a few hundred dollars. Not even me.

I don't advertise myself as a "shaman" or healer of any kind. I am aware that at times I am performing healing work, that for some, the process itself is ritual and meaningful. Tattoos are incredibly meaningful and important- but they're not necessary. I don't think I could live up to the responsibility implied by the word "healer". I'm not an actual priestess. But I try very hard to let that energy exist in my work when I feel that it's possible.

It's just possible a lot less often these days.

I think this shift in expectations, from then til now, has made me more withdrawn, more reclusive. I know that I am harder to reach for tattoos now than I ever have been before. That the process of getting me to tattoo you is more difficult, more drawn-out. That I no longer am in a hurry.

I think it is a good thing. I think I do better at the tattoos that I make now, than I have before. And I think it makes me more able to connect with my clients than I had been recently.

Conventions.

I've worked a lot of conventions, and guest spots, and traveled for work in general. To all my past, present, and future boyfriends, girlfriends, houseboys, significant others, and just plain others:

I go to work.

That's right. Guest spots are fun. Travel is a great time. Conventions? A big party. But I'm working. I work there. I'm not going to just "hang out" or "party time" or anything like that. I'm promoting myself, my shop, my work. I'm selling prints (sometimes with your help!) I'm tattooing. I'm entering contests. I'm working, the whole time. The afterparty? Just a way for me to find out how to re-attach a tube vise.

I know it seems glamorous from the perspective of new people, friends, and places. From the outside it sure looks like I'm just enjoying a perk of the job. But I'm not- it IS the job.

If I don't bring you to a show it's not necessarily because I want to get laid. It's not because I want you to have no fun. Usually, it's because I can't have you standing in the booth all day, hanging out. I'm working. There's no room there. Unless it's a town in which there's tons to do and that you will be doing besides the convention, you're in the way most of the time. You're not going to work the booth, are you? talk to everyone that walks by? go get me a coffee while I draw for the next guy? rub my shoulders when they hurt? No?

Then what are you doing at my work? You're not working. For you it IS just the big party. I don't usually mind you going along but there are things I need to do that are harder with you there- talk shop, for one. Fit two clients and their friends into a 10×10 space. Work and network without being interrupted or asked questions. NOT ARGUE while I am trying to network with my colleagues.

kat von d, fame, and talent

People who become famous through "reality" tv are not always prepared for the backlash. They're not necessarily the best in their field, just people who are pretty good at what they do and who look good on camera.

I'm also a woman who tattoos. I can't tell you how many people ask me about her- it's as if she is the touchstone for outsiders, as if being a woman and a tattoo artist means I have some deep interest in her.

The unfortunate thing about this is that I don't watch reality tv at all; also, I don't do anything remotely like her work. I work with an artist who does very good black and grey and portrait work. I don't. I do mostly color work, large color work...I think people just assume I will be like her in more ways than I am.

Also, I've been tattooing as long as she has. I wonder how many people realize that what they see on television is not always going to be true to real life. I've always disliked reality-style television, mainly because it blurs the line in a way that I feel is dishonest. Most of the people appearing on reality television are not living their normal, day-to-day lives. They've got a script, they're working as actors on television, not working in the job that's being portrayed. At least, while the cameras are rolling, they are. And that makes things look a bit different. Being in the chair is a lot different than watching someone else sit there.

I have a lot of sympathy for her. It must be hard in a lot of ways to be in everyone's eyes all the time. I wouldn't want to be that famous, that way- I get nervous sometimes just having one other artist watching me, let alone all of them! every little slip, mistake, tiny error magnified for your peers to pick apart and hate you for- it must be tough.

I do dislike the fact that whenever I see her featured in a tattoo magazine there are rarely good photographs of her WORK. I have seen her face in other magazines, and that's fine, but in an industry publication I want to see her work. As an actor she's pretty attractive... but as a tattoo artist I have no idea. I so rarely get the opportunity to judge her work the same way I judge the work of my true peers, by seeing it in context, presented alongside the work of other tattooers. I'd like it if at least within our own industry's purview (like the trade magazines) we could focus on what she does, not how she looks while she's doing it.

Seeing her face and her bikini line doesn't tell me a damn thing about how good she is as an artist; it's also sexist. And this is the thing that bothers me.

prank wars.

Someone brought two whoopee cushions into the shop the other day.

If you have ever worked in a tattoo shop, you know how hard it is to maintain a prank-free zone. For some reason tattooers, more than any other occupation I have ever heard of, have a serious problem with prank wars. I cannot count the number of times I have had whole days of wearing gentian violet mustaches, stencil ink headbands, or even had blue ink powder on the crotch of my pants. And this is just the basic harmless day-to-day stuff-

In fact, every prank war ends the same way; with human feces, elk urine, or sore knuckles. While the emotional state of the participants at the end always depends on how close everyone was at the start, and on the sense of humor of those involved, it's true that there will eventually be poop and someone will get hit. I've seen friendships ruined in prank wars but more often I've seen people with a black eye laughing their ass off with the perpetrator the next day at the bar.

Keep in mind, nothing I've ever seen personally was dangerous to anyone involved. Nor have I ever seen anyone break or destroy or make unsafe, any work equipment. I've seen people put tape over a contact point on a machine so it won't run until the tape's removed…but never have I seen anyone do anything risky to themselves or others in this context. Just…ridiculous things.

So when the whoopee cushions appeared I looked forward in time with my prophetic eye and said "This will all end in shit."

I remember one shop I worked at where the pranks escalated over the course of a summer. Started with someone bringing in fake puke- you know, that plastic stuff you get at the dollar store on the "novelty rack". Funny. It was left on someone's counter for them to find the next day.

Two days later the victim of this small joke put beet powder in the guy's food-pasta sauce. This guy was known for waiting to relieve himself until we were all working, and then stinking up the bathroom at the shop. Horrible really, but a funny habit he had. The next day, he called me into the bathroom. "Anj, I don't know what to do. Should I call a doctor? I'm kind of scared." He pointed to the bowl. Sometimes, being completely non-judgemental about people's problems gives me the opportunity to see some amazing things.

He'd shit what looked like blood. I started laughing- I'd been there when the beet powder was applied to the bowl in the fridge. I said, very calmly, "Have you been having some rough anal lately?"

The guy was terrified. He went out to talk to the boss (who had also seen the beet powder stunt). The boss took pity and told him.

A few days later the original victim was seen walking around with black smudges on his face, all around his mouth. Hair dye on his coffee mug. His entire chin was black. That stuff actually dyes your skin and will not wash off. His chin faded to an orange-brown by the next day and it lingered for almost a week.

Of course by that time, things had become more serious.

By the end, when human poop was left on someone's car hood and someone else had been punched in the face, everyone at the shop was heartily sick of it. Except for me. I wasn't involved but I'd been following gleefully the whole time...and I have had my fair share of prank wars of my own. They demand a certain sense of humor to enjoy, and not everyone has it. (insert *real bronx cheer* here)

I've enjoyed the few years we have had since the surgical staple gun replica broke. But I guess I always knew that this industry has its flavor and pranking is the major spice involved.

Dave.

I was tattooing a woman, and her husband was holding her hand and talking to her through it. She passed out, and, as some people are wont to do, mumbled and wiggled while she was out. She mumbled a name, "Dave". The husband immediately got up and left.

She came to a few seconds later, and asked where he was. I said, well he went outside. She gets on her phone to call him and ask him to come back inside, and I get to hear the conversation...

He's left her there with no ride home. Apparently "Dave" is a guy he thought she might be cheating with, and her saying it while she was passed out was just further confirmation.

She cried, but got her tattoo finished. Awkward as hell for me. And yes- the guy who eventually came and picked her up? Dave.

tattoo motivation

There are tattoo artists out there who have never worked in a studio without being asked about a TV show.

The demand for tattoos, good tattoos, and the number of people tattooing, makes this a completely different subculture than it was when I started out.

Does this mean the magic is gone? Am I no longer a wizard? Did reality TV really eat the soul of tattooing? Maybe a year or two ago I would have said yes, and ranted for a while about it. But right now- No. I don't think the soul is gone, we are still wizards, and the magic is still there, and as potent as ever.

You can't do much worse than sell the soul of your work and try to make it popular, AND be upset when you are done cashing your check.

I can understand why, if you sold the soul of your work to the masses, you might worry about the dilution of your wizardry. And you don't have to suck, or be an asshole, to sell out. People sell out all the time, and we all have different prices. I mean shit- I've had work published in magazines, I've apprenticed one person, I've worked in street shops doing lettuce and tribble all day. I'll do "breathe" in white on a wrist without even blinking.

But I won't try to popularize or explain the methods of tattooing to the mainstream. That's my limit, that's where I draw a line (well, that and letting pictures of ME instead of MY WORK get published. but that's more a feminist thing)

When I go to work there's magic. In handling people's skins, looking into their eyes, joking with them, marking them. Just because the masses now like and get tattoos does not dilute the power of each individual tattoo for its wearer. Just because there are more tattoo artists does not make any one tattoo less important or interesting in a general sense- after all, there are no cameras watching me work, watching the person sit for it. They say cameras can steal your soul, you know? I can't mass-produce tattoos. Tattoos, by their very nature, are private and individual. Shining a spotlight on them sucks out the magic from THAT TATTOO, from THAT artist- not from the rest of us.

And as far as new/old tattoo artists go- I was new at one time. I think good artists are rare, in any medium, and tattooing can always use GOOD, CREATIVE people- who also have the mentality and dedication to work with people properly, who live up to some of the old ways.

You should know how to do everything, even if you don't do it regularly- how to make needles, build and repair machines, mix inks, wind coils, draw, do your bills and taxes, scrub tubes, cut a stencil. These things may not be necessary, but they're important. They are the secret magical lore of our trade.

I never expected tattooing to be glamorous, and I had never heard of anyone quitting tattooing to do some other work, when I started. Now, I know there are people who have both an expectation of glamor, and a sense of entitlement to learning to tattoo. While I personally disapprove of tattoo "schools" and people apprenticing more than one or two people during their career, that's not my call to make for everyone else. All I can say is that like any profession, you aren't entitled to know how to do this. You should have to work hard to learn it. And you should be the one to initiate learning everything. Everything! All the secret lore, all the hidden tricks.

Teaching yourself never has cut it; it doesn't give you what you need to do good tattoos.

Going to a "school" and then opening your own shop because nobody local will hire you is NOT going to cut it- your exposure to other artists is what shows you how to do things, not thinking you've learned it all.

I won't preach humility, though. Because being good at drawing already makes you a wizard to most people! Your skills and talents are necessary and important in tattooing. Use them! Tattooing is specialized knowledge. Watching a TV show teaches nothing. Nobody can learn to tattoo from that. So even though clients now like to present themselves as somehow "in the know" from watching TV, they AREN'T. We're the wizards, and they come to us for magic.

We shouldn't let them down.

Knuckle sandwich

TATTOOING

on drawing flash.

Most tattooers draw some flash, at least once, somewhere along the line. It's common to start trying to draw flash when you realize that you've accumulated a big pile of sketches that you haven't tattooed yet, thinking, "I could make a flash set, or a sketchbook, out of all this stuff."

This is a trap.

Flash sets are more useful when they can be used. The art that someone didn't want on them isn't going to sell very well, to artists, or by artists to clients. Flash should be easy, fun, and reproducible- that's what it's for.

Think about the end user- the tattoo artist who will have to reproduce what you've done on someone's skin. Did you include lots of finicky little lines that are not backed up by any background? Well, it's a sure thing some wiggly-ass newcomer is going to want that impossible thing on their wobbly love handles. Have you ever tried to tattoo a thin, long line on that? I'm sure you hated it just as much as any other artist would.

So avoid those kind of things in your flash. Make your drawings simple, bold, and easy to apply.

Think about the size and complexity of your art, too. That big full-sheet drawing of a wicked dragon? Well, most tattoo artists will do something on that scale as CUSTOM work anyway. The client may glance at your flash and say "Something like that" but the artist isn't going to want to invest hours upon hours into copying your work. As a matter of fact, he's probably not going to buy your set, and it's unlikely that if he does he'll want to hang that on his wall. He might even get disgruntled if someone DOES ask for that piece!

So draw smaller things, the things you don't even feel like drawing-draw the things that it's a pain in the ass to have to draw for someone.

Did you just assemble a set of new skool art-related stuff, like spray cans, pencils, and the like? Guess who likes that stuff? That's right-other tattooers. Same goes for old-school style pigfishicorns, and bloody severed hands. Guess who doesn't like that stuff and won't pick it off the wall? That's right, tattoo clients. Most tattooers won't end up doing flash on each other- they want to draw. In the 21st century, most tattooers are artists first and foremost. While it can be argued whether or not this is a good thing, it can't be argued that these days flash is a little bit useless, to many artists.

Draw with them in mind.

You yourself are probably one of these people- so if it's something you wish you had a copy of, because you hate re-drawing it, then most likely it's the kind of thing that will go over well on flash.

If you think about it, the things that are small, spontaneous, impulse tattoos are what flash is made for. That's the stuff that works on the wall. The world doesn't have enough well-drawn, well-planned, easily-applied celtic knots smaller than 6? across, butterflies that are simplistic without being a fucking joke, panther heads that are majestic and not goofy-looking. The world has more than enough sailor jerry pin-up ripoffs, skulls with various things crossed behind them, etc etc etc

The things you love to draw? Well, paint them. Make a nice 8×10? painting of them, and sell prints. Don't try to pass these off as flash.

Think about the easiest way to tattoo something. What can you do to make the piece easier for the artist? Breaking up long lines, keeping plenty of space between lines or dark areas, using high contrast...these help. How would YOU want to tattoo it? What would make it quicker or easier for YOU?

Of course if you don't tattoo, none of this helps at all. You can't draw on your own experience, your own difficulties, your own knowledge of skin and the way it reacts to different techniques. As tattooers, we have a unique perspective on art. The things other artists see as "simple" are often the very hardest to pull of on a squirming bit of flesh, while what is hard on canvas is sometimes the easiest thing in the world.

I see a lot of wonky tribble, tightly packed noodly stuff, that is just impossible to tattoo, from outsiders. I'd never in my life buy flash that looked like that...

Once you've got a theme for your set (think of one! I once did a thanksgiving set...once I did a set of watery stuff...it should all fit together somewhat in the viewer's mind) decide how many pages you're aiming for. five, six, ten, and twelve....I have seen. Less than five pages is not a set. More than twelve is out of most artists' price range.

Then start assembling the art. I usually draw freely until I have a huge stack of sketches. Then I transfer them to 11×14 paper, bristol or watercolor paper, and begin coloring and lining. I have a bad habit of forgetting to do a line sheet until after I've colored- learn from my mistake!

Try to leave "breathing room" between pieces on each sheet. By this I do not mean leave half the page blank- no, you should place the pieces no more than a half inch from each other. You want to give the artist their money's worth, but not make the page look cluttered.

Printing can be as cheap or as nice as you like. In the end, it all depends on what crowd you're aiming for.

I've found that shops that are less packed with experienced talent, and shops with older owners, and shops with lots of younger artists, are the three best buyers of flash. The shops in which people are less artistically inclined need your flash, they can make money by purchasing it, and they will actually use it. This is a good feeling. This is why your art should be easy to understand and apply, when you draw flash. Guy Aitchison doesn't need your help- Joe Schmoe down the road, however, really appreciates it.

The older artists are accustomed to buying flash, and like it. Some of these older guys have amazing collections of flash. To them it is an investment. If your art is good and simple they will eat it up.

Younger artists often use flash for reference or ideas, also they haven't the ability, often, to pull a koi out of their ass. This is where you come in. By looking at what you have drawn, and seeing it made simple, they can learn from what you've done. If you are one of the younger set, you can learn a lot by drawing flash. It may not sell very well, but you will have learned a lot by the time you're finished.

tattoo composition.

Composition is the science of combination. It's learning how to draw the viewer's eye exactly where you want it to go, in and through your artwork. With tattooing, composition is probably the most important aspect of the work. Flow and antiflow are key to both the success of a tattoo, and the wearer's appreciation of your work.

When you start putting together a tattoo drawing, the very first and most important thing you should think about is the structure of the body underneath it. Think about whether the area will distort, stretch, or bend, making the image look incorrect; about whether the image's direction will fight the engineering of the musculature it will be tattooed on.

Guy Aitchison has some excellent diagrams of this principle in his book "Reinventing the Tattoo", if you don't already own this book I'd strongly suggest you get a copy. It's available at his website, if you are a professional artist.

For example, let's say you are doing a tattoo that is pretty common, a piece on the inside of the wearer's forearm. from the knob of the wrist under the pinky, to the outside of the elbow, is a diagonal line of flow that represents the muscle structure underneath the skin. The force of the forearm muscle is made to curve this way so that you can turn your hand palm up or palm down. That is the biggest muscle in the area, and you can see it bulge up over the top of the elbow into the bicep. It's an important part of the arm, this area, very visible.

So look at your own forearm on the inside. If you have a marker handy, draw a line from below your pinky by your wrist, to the outside of your elbow ditch. There's the basis of your flow.

Also this area is a long, thin oval (for most people). If you have paper, draw a long oval on it, with that diagonal line across it showing where that muscle goes. Now you have a compositional beginning. You know where you want their eye to move through the design, and if you can convince their eye to follow that curved diagonal across the arm, you'll have made that arm look more attractive.

Anton Lavey said that the basic most attractive shape to the human eye is the S curve. He was right. A looping double curve draws our eye in, seducing it gently, making us want to see more. Think of the classic two-handed s-curve of the old cartoons, which makes the silhouette of a voluptuous woman. This is the kind of seduction we want to unleash on the viewer's eye.

It doesn't matter what the subject of the tattoo will be, what colors, or anything at this point. Composition is the science of combination-you're going to combine the general shapes of the design into something attractive, that fits the form under it, in order to make a pleasing composition for the tattoo. You can plug any subject or object into a good composition and it will retain its strength.

If you want something very abrupt and masculine, try using a right angle instead of a curve. Squaring off curves within a composition makes it more jagged, more macho, more sudden and abrupt. The viewer's eye will stop short at each corner, before continuing, so make sure there is something interesting there for it to rest on.

Leave some areas for the eye to rest. Cramming a wealth of detail into a piece just makes it confusing to look at- pick the important part of the composition, and do your high-impact detail there, and nowhere else. This way the person looking at the piece will be drawn right in to the most dramatic and awesome part of the tattoo, without feeling overwhelmed or confused.

freehand/tracing.

When I get someone who wants something done on an awkward part of their body, I encounter a tracing dilemma. See, I personally find it easier and less stress-inducing to just do a few thumbnails and then draw with marker onto skin the day of their appointment.

This costs a bit more in time, because I don't charge them for this drawing time, but it takes the pressure off me to draw something that will fit three dimensions, on a two-dimensional paper. There ARE ways to do it, though. Not necessarily secret ways, just ways to make tracing an area easier for everyone involved.

I like to use contact paper- transparent sticky-backed paper. cut it, cut it out to fit the shape of the body. Sometimes this means cutting notches out of the edges so it will curve. trace all the overlaps with a red sharpie so you know what's skin and what's layers of the paper.

Then with a black sharpie trace the muscles, the outside edge you want the piece to stay within. Mark the limits of the piece. Mark the flow of the body. Note if it's right or left. Which muscle is defined and which isn't. weird moles or hairy patches. You know, take notes.

From this I'll take tracing paper and make my sketches.

But usually….usually I prefer to draw on skin. I'll sometimes take a photo of the area, a picture of the person. And print it out in black and whihte on crappy paper. then lay trace paper over that photo and sketch what I think might look right.

These sketches are tiny, nowhere near actual size, but they are just blueprints, just plans. I bring all the photo or other reference on the day of, along with these sketches, and I use them to draw from.

Some people can't handle the uncertainty of not seeing the tattoo beforehand. They wanna go home and consider the art, etc etc… I turn these people away. They are good people, just not the kind who will be happy with my process. They might even really like what I do but if they can't hang with the process I use to get the results I get, then they simply can't get worked on by me. I work how I work, and if they like the end result they have to understand that I get there by following MY process, MY flow…there's just no other way I can do it.

Most people are fine with that, the ones that aren't…well shit, I don't have to be everyone's artist. There are plenty of good artists to go around.

apprenticeships.

My standard advice to anyone wanting to learn to tattoo is "MOVE OUT OF OREGON AND GET A REAL APPRENTICESHIP". I find the idea of "schools" laughable and repugnant.

You simply cannot teach "class" of more than one person hands-on, tattooing is not like other fields in this sense. Apprenticeships served one-on-one, by the person who plans to hire you afterward, are and were the tattoo industry standard.

Being here is the first time I have ever heard of a tattoo "school" being taken seriously by ANYONE as anything but a scam that teaches the student nothing.

Churning out people without being responsible for their future career is a terrible idea; I'd never before heard of ANYONE being taught without being hired by the teacher once they'd learned.

An artist who is very skilled and dedicated does not have time or interest in teaching twenty people. They may take the time to properly apprentice one or two during their career. In order for an artist like this to have an apprentice in Oregon, they must open a school in a manner that assumes they will want to teach multiple people; they must charge money, they must do a lot of things which deters them from bothering at all. The system in Oregon is set up so that the very best tattoo artists won't teach, and those with less skill, will.

People who are proficient at filling out forms and such; not good tattooers. We end up with under-educated people with no place to work, turned loose to fend for themselves.

I feel like a lot of these younger artists were completely ripped off by the system, taken advantage of, their ambitions falsely turned against them. We could have so many highly-trained young artists here, instead we have a pile of people who COULD be great, but are flailing around trying to learn on their own. It's a waste of time, and it's bad for tattooing.

Again- you can NOT teach tattooing in a class. This requires apprenticeship and mentoring beyond that; should be done in the interest of furthering our art, not raking in cash from naive starry-eyed kids and then tossing them out in the street to beg for work (or worse, open their own shop because they can't find a job...how are they going to learn more then? When they are working alone with only their limited knowledge to go on?)

A few people have done the best they can teaching under these rules, but a first-year OR tattoo artist is still, STILL, light-years behind almost any other first-year tattooer.

In tattooing, it's not good form to talk down on whoever taught you, no matter how fucked-up things ended, or how poorly the teaching as done. I feel that the current rules in oregon were passed without any insight into the general standards of tattooing nationwide and have really made us look bad in comparison to other places. The school/apprentice thing being the biggest issue.

It's not so much the number of new artists, because demand is still high and rising. it's the quality and skill of those artists! YOU SHOULD NOT TEACH SOMEONE YOU DON'T PLAN TO HIRE. simply put!

The input given by a mentor during the first few years of tattooing is just as important as the original apprenticeship, and a formal apprenticeship gives in-depth, hands-on information that can't be given in a class setting, or by someone who is teaching a herd.

For you guys who are wanting to learn tattooing. MOVE OUT OF OREGON. If you have other things in your life preventing that, be aware that YOU WILL NOT HAVE TIME FOR THOSE THINGS ANYWAY. The time during your apprenticeship, tattooing needs to be the first and only priority in your life.

So, move! Find someone who wants to INVEST in you, share their knowledge, and guide you. Don't slap down cash on the barrelhead and expect to be a respected artist because you bought in.

youth and tattoo rebellion

There are a lot of younger people today who are very interested in tattoos. In many cultures tattoos are used as a rite of passage from youth to adulthood, and in our Western culture it is no different. The lack of culturally-based rites of passage and tests of maturity leads many teenagers to seek alternate forms of self-challenge, and tattooing is currently high on that list.

Children are only tattooed usually by indigenous or tribal groups to whom it is a cultural staple. Occasionally there will be a photograph of a child wearing airbrushed tattoos (which are painted on) in a magazine, but actual children are extremely rarely tattooed.

Although most jurisdictions outlaw the tattooing of minors, many children and teenagers will tattoo themselves at home, using sewing or other needles and common household dyes and inks. This can be extremely dangerous; using an unsterilized needle or one that has been used on another person can transmit disease or cause serious infections. Home-made tattoos tend to be deeper in the skin surface than professional tattoos, and this can lead to infections that cause excessive scarring. Most commonly found dyes and inks in home use are not inert and can cause allergic reactions or other problems. Young people should NOT use household items to tattoo themselves; this is a given. That they WILL do it, is incontestable. Educating young people and explaining to them that sharing needles (no matter what sort of home "sterilization" they invent)can transmit HIV, hepatitis, and bacterial infections, is a good beginning; also it may help to explain that running a needle through flame, boiling it, or soaking it in alcohol or antibacterial wipes will not kill all bacteria or viruses that may be present.

Since minors can not obtain a legal tattoo, they will often try to use fake ID to do so. Parents should be aware that professional studios are not pleased about this; parents should always attempt to contact the studio where their child claims to have received a tattoo. Studios often are required by law to keep consent forms for up to two years, and can usually provide a copy of the false identification that was used. This is not usually negligence by the studio, but fraud by the minor. In some states the studio can prosecute the minor and their parent. Parents should make sure that their teenagers have no access to their wallets and purses.

When a teenager is nearing eighteen and the age of consent, parents should do research with them into studios they may frequent or patronize. It may be reassuring for parents to know that the studio is clean and reputable. Minors are often not welcome in tattoo studios without a parent; this can be a good opportunity for parents to ensure that if their teenager decides to get tattooed they are at least in a situation that is not unsafe or unhealthy.

Parents should know that every shop should have an autoclave which is regularly spore tested, disposable latex or nitrile gloves should be used, and all workers there have proper health and safety training.

Bringing your teenager with you to investigate their options may also discourage them from performing unsafe tattoos on themselves at home, and may even dissuade them from getting a rebellion-motivated tattoo at all. After all, if parents approve, many teens won't participate.

getting coverups.

Unfortunately, laser removal is the closest thing to the magic eraser, and it is expensive and painful, some say more painful than tattoos.

Getting a coverup is a common solution. Here are a few easy things you can do to make sure you don't make the same mistake twice-

Pretend you have no bad tattoo. Imagine a peaceful world in which that tattoo never even existed. Now, picture a good tattoo on the area. What does it look like? Hint- it will NEVER be a current lover's name, or the same as the old one but smaller. Got it? Good. That's your goal. Keep that image in your mind throughout these steps.

Find an artist. Look at every tattoo shop and website you can find. Shop around- at shops. Don't go to someone's basement or home to get tattooed. Look at professional artists only. It will cost some money, since coverups take longer to do, but it will be worth it to get rid of the old mistake.

Look at all the portfolios you can, and pick up a few tattoo magazines. Who is doing something that is similar to the style of your imaginary tattoo? Try to find someone whose work resembles what you're picturing as your new tattoo. Don't look at the subject matter, look at the style. Look at the color choices, placement, and way of drawing. If you like it, it is good. This is your personal art collection, and your taste is all that matters.

Talk to an artist. For coverups, you will most likely have to go in person to the studio and talk to the artist. Getting a firsthand look at the problem is the only way they can find a solution. Listen to what they have to say; take it into account. They cover up old tattoos often and will probably have some good advice for you about your particular situation.

Coverups must usually be much larger than the old tattoo. They also must have at least some areas of shadow to hide any pre-existing dark areas. Tattoo inks are translucent, and a paler color will eventually let a darker one underneath it show through.

This does not mean your coverup has to be all black. "Tribal" designs are actually a very poor choice for a coverup design, as they rely on areas of smoothly curving negative space to be attractive to the eye. The negative space is empty skin, and usually it takes a lot of work to coordinate this negative space in a design with what is already present.

You will not usually find a design ready-made to cover up your tattoo. Remember, it can come up through lighter colors. Your artist will have to draw something specifically designed to hide your previous work. This may take time, so be patient. They may want to trace the area so they can use reference to draw on at home, or they may suggest freehand work.

Freehand coverups done by good artists are the best solution to covering up an old unwanted tattoo. By drawing directly on the skin (drawing is done first with marker, then tattooed on) the artist can take into account the form of the old tattoo, as well as your anatomy.

The most important step in the entire process is finding the right artist. Look for someone you like, whose art you admire. Try to find an artist who enjoys not only coverups but also really appreciates the same kind of artwork that you do. Since all coverups are custom tattoos drawn by the tattoo artist, make sure the artist you pick has the same kind of taste you do.

Coverups can be very expensive. Tattoo artists know that if you had valued your personal canvas, and their artform, you wouldn't need one! Be sure to tip well when getting a coverup done. Most artists spend more effort and time drawing for coverups than they would drawing an original tattoo, and most don't charge anything for their drawing time. Be aware of this extra work they've done and tip accordingly.

You can't get a coverup on the spur of the moment, unless it is so tiny that it's hardly visible to begin with. You'll have to plan in advance and think quite a bit about your new tattoo. Hasty decisions are the reason coverups exist in the first place, so take your time and do some research before you buy.

Getting a coverup may limit your choices in some ways, but the subject matter and style is still wide open. Knowing that it may have to be darker and larger should not keep you from getting a tattoo you can be proud of, and if you find the right artist you may even forget the old tattoo was there. If you can picture what you want, you can find a way to make it work, as long as you find someone who is capable of tackling the job.

soul to the surface.

Most people avoid pain at all costs.

Most people, that is, who don't work out, diet, wear makeup or high heels, or get tattooed. The phrase "no pain, no gain" is as apt with tattooing as with any other uncomfortable act people perform for a better reward. The profit, in this case, a permanent decoration, outweighs the discomfort.

Tattoos, while painful, are not distressingly so. The pain results from surface nerves in the upper layer of skin and the hair follicles being punctured or pressed on by a group of small, hair-fine needles inserted rapidly about 1-2 mm into the skin.

Tattoo needles in a typical tattoo machine move in and out so rapidly that they can't be seen in motion, only as a blur. The sensation is not like punctures or pokes, but more like a continuous tingling scratch. Most of the damage to the skin is from the friction of the needles' motion.

During a tattoo, sensations range from mild and almost dull to very sharp and intense. When the process first begins, the body responds strongly to the sensations, releasing endorphins (the same hormones that cause a "runner's high") and adrenalin. Adrenalin can cause a fight-or-flight response, making the process very uncomfortable at the beginning.

Once the endorphins are absorbed by the system, however, the sensations rapidly become duller and less urgent. The pain may be just as unpleasant, but becomes less intense and attention-grabbing. This is the stage some people refer to as "numbing". Some people even fall asleep during this stage of a tattoo.

The endorphin rush associated with getting tattooed, or with running marathons, is notorious for becoming addictive. It is the same internal reaction that's mimicked by the drug ecstasy and morphine, among others.

Endorphins cause a warm inner glow, like that caused by running or tanning. They block the body's pain receptors, so while they're in the system other pains (like a sore back, or previous injury) are also diminished. They also flood the brain with dopamines, which allow the body to recover from injury by relaxing. This after-tattoo "buzz" more than makes up for the previous pain for many people, and can account for the addictiveness of tattooing.

People who are getting their first tattoo have usually weighed the pros and cons, and are interested enough in the personal expression to be gained by applying the image to deal with some level of pain. It is for most a planned decision; and most tattooed people will say that the first tattoo they acquired hurt much less than they'd anticipated.

So why, if they think it will be so painful, would they still get it done? Most would say it's because they wanted the tattoo badly enough not to care. Some are seeking personal pride in having conquered the pain, using mind-over-matter as a test of their willpower or inner strength. Others are already adept at dealing with physical pain, and don't see it as an obstacle at all; and a very small group actually enjoy pain. In ten years as a professional and busy tattoo artist, I've only met two of these out of thousands of clients.

Some say pain is change resisted, or that pain is growth, or that beauty is suffering. In short, people are willing to suffer in order to look the way they'd like to look. They will deal with some pain in order to bring their soul to the surface.

Knuckle sandwich

ARTS

working with oil paints.

I tend to paint in an enclosed room.
Yes, I know. I know this is bad, and you're supposed to air out the
    turpentine, and the chemicals, and the smell. You're also not
        supposed to:
taste your paint to see if it's the right color
lick your brush tip to straighten it out or check dampness
rub the paint onto the canvas with your fingers
especially if you are eating a sandwich while painting
actually you're not supposed to eat while you work, are you?
oh shit, that wasn't the turp it was my coffee
whatever, I don't want to get up and get more
what is that buzzing noise, anyway
I can say that I have probably done more damage to my brain cells
by enjoying my work too much to get up and walk into another room
for anything else, including food, than I have ever damaged with liquor
or stupid stunts.

And I used to drink until I couldn't remember which direction to
walk to get home, and give people mean headbutts as a show of
affection. So…Air out your studio. Get up and leave the room to eat and
have coffee. Don't eat paint.

If you are anything like me you've been told this before and simply ignored it.

I'm not going to presume to give you any horror stories about this kind of weirdness. but that's only because the worst thing that's ever happened to me from behaving this way is oily-tasting coffee.

That and the occasional headache.

photo reference.

We all know how boring it can get to see the same few poses, faces, or roses tattooed again and again. It's a strange ethical question in some ways- is a still from a film, a figure model on the internet, or a flower you find on google, stolen property if you trace/redraw slightly, and tattoo it?

You can start fixing this by beginning to create your own photo reference library. If you have a relatively decent camera, whether or not it's digital (although digital is easier, and what I'll be discussing here) you can acquire a lot of reference that nobody else has access to.

Photograph everything. Get a big memory card- it's a write-off- and start taking pictures of the flowers in your garden, ask your friends to pose for you. Have them stand and sit in different positions and make different faces, different emotions and moods. Just be sure to organize your pictures by subject, not by date! That way you can always find "red rose bud" in the mass of pictures you will end up with.

This brings originality to your work, while allowing you to stay fairly true to life. If you plan to specialize in photorealistic or "color zombie portrait head" style work, you'd better start shooting now, because if I see another devil's rejects stillframe #13892 again I will scream.

color theory.

It's strange to me, that the color theory classes I took back in the day never mentioned much about the symbolic meaning of colors. It was very cut-and-dried, physics information...which is something I needed to learn, of course, and still use all the time...but it would be nice to combine both color theory on a physical level with color theory on a symbolic level.

Like I often use brown and red, up against black, then put light blue behind it. The reds and the browns have more warmth up against a cold pale blue...something I've noticed when looking at bricks in the early pale morning light, up against a blue grey sky. But those colors- it's the meaning that makes it an interesting combination. Coldness and freedom, loyalty, and the home/hearth...my backgrounds are free but my foregrounds are rooted.

Working with browns and subdued or neutral colors

Browns, and neutral tones, can be hard to work with on skin. Skin itself is made up of many different undertones of color, and sometimes more subdued color can almost get lost on the surface.

Some tricks that help make it work include:

Using enough black in the shadowed areas. Make sure that the dark-to-light ratio is strong, and contrast is high throughout the piece.

Using varying hues. Try to incorporate both yellowy and purplish browns. Or if you are using olive greens, also use some strong maroon in the shadow areas.

Make sure you're mixing the colors down from the bottle. Using a straight bottle brown often ends in dull, washed out color. Adding a bit of red, purple, green, or blue will make your browns richer.

Get up and away from the skin. Stand up and walk a few steps back if you start getting lost in the color blends. Wipe it down and look at it from more than a few inches away. You should be able to see the gradation better from a distance.

Don't be afraid of white. Mixing white into your brown will often show you which color you need to add to mute it, or strengthen it.

Browns, technically speaking, are simply very dull tones of another color. Many of the browns we see daily in life are actually oranges that have a lot of muddying in them. Sienna is a reddish, or orangey brown used by painters. Ochre is a yellowish brown, and umber is a purplish color, but is closest to a "true" brown in color.

If you want something to look shadowed, often adding a bit of blue to the brown will cool it off. It may dull other colors to a muddy brown, but this often works to show areas of cold shadow.

Grey is another subject entirely. I will address toned grey here briefly.

When using greys in a piece that has a foreground and a background which overlap, it can sometimes help your depth to use a tiny bit of blue in the background grey, and the tiniest bit of umber ("chocolate" brown, in tattoo ink terms) in the grey of the foreground. This adds warmth to the objects that are meant to be closer.

Basic color theory states that an object which is approaching will look warmer than a receding object. This has to do with physics, but suffice it to say that due to atmospheric effects it usually holds true, that our eyes will subconsciously perceive something warm in color as closer to us than something cold in color.

Using beige, white, and tan in a tattoo is not often useful. Most skin is either within the same color range, or too dark for these tones to work well. If you get lucky enough to work on someone very pale, you can use these colors for highlights or accents. Using the neutral beige and tan as highlights in areas of the piece that are meant to look further away, and reserving the use of white for only a few small select areas, can help you draw the viewer's eye into one area of the composition.

If you use white do so sparingly, keeping in mind that using consistent brightness throughout a piece makes it look "flat"; vary the strength of your highlights to add emphasis to an area, or make it look closer or more important.

preserving certain specimens.

How to clean animal remains you find that still have a bit of meat on them:

Wear disposable gloves.

Put them on a piece of window screen that is twice their size, and wrap them up in it. Fold over the edges to close it like a pocket, leaving a one inch opening on one end for flies and other insects to get in.

DO NOT BOIL OR SIMMER BONES. Cooked bones can and will ROT! Boiling breaks the fibers that hold bone together, making them brittle, and thinning them. Let nature do the work for you! (and keep the stink outside!)

Hang the corpse-pocket up outside. You want it up out of reach of cats and dogs, but low enough that you can reach it. I hang remains from a tree limb near my house. You can also wrap the corpse this was and then bury it a foot deep or less. Either way, insects will do the cleaning for you. This will not work in winter though.

wait a few weeks, less if it is hot/humid. check on your developments. at some point the bones will be fully exposed, and all meat will have been picked away by insects.

soak the bones in HOT water and blue Dawn dish detergent. Change out the water/detergent mix every day. It can cool off overnight, just use hot water to refill it each day. Use about two cups of Dawn per gallon of water. Do this until the bones are not yellowish with fat anymore.

Scrub the bones in cold water with more dish soap. Then soak again in HOT water, mixed 1:1 with regular old store-type peroxide. YOU DON'T NEED BLEACH; BLEACH WILL MAKE THE BONE CRUMBLY AND WEAK, AND SOFTEN IT. Peroxide and hot water will disinfect just as well, when used in conjunction with the soap soak. refill/continue soaking until the bone is as white as you'd like. I find that it usually takes three water changes to get the ivory-cream tone I prefer.

Dry the bones thoroughly, NOT IN THE SUN. Then spray with a coat of matte UV protectant. Sun exposure, like bleach, degrades and weakens bone.

The best way to hang a skull is to string it on thick, soft twine through the orbital bones, then hang that on a hook on a mounting board. I like to attach the jaw as well, and pose and articulate bones- I'll go over that stuff in a later post.

DON'T FUCKING BOIL OR BLEACH BONES! IT DESTROYS THEM!

How to disinfect feathers (legal ones- domestic and game birds)

Wear disposable gloves.

Figure out if it is a land or water bird. Water birds have oil in their feathers, land birds do not.

Spray with alcohol(land bird) or tea tree oil (water bird) and let dry.

Soak a paper towel with full-strength hand sanitizer, and wipe feather gently, in the direction of growth. Soak the feather well.

Let stand overnight.

Using hot water, wipe the feather down again. Let dry. Use oil or a damp cloth to smooth the feather to shape it again.

To dye land-bird feathers, use translucent, lightfast inks (FW, or the like) and wipe ink onto feather surfaces in the pattern you want. let it stand until the ink has dried, then wipe gently with a damp rag.

To dye waterbird feathers, translucent oil paints in minute amounts, or oil-based wood stain both work very well.

BONES AND SUCH.

I want to talk a little bit about my materials. Mainly because I read a lot of forums and craft and art blogs, and tend to see the same comments over and over about artists that work with taxidermy or animal remains.

Nature isn't cruel or kind; it's just hungry.

I get a lot of questions about various things I use- mostly about bones and skulls, but a lot of people have asked about other things too- plants, rocks. Usually people are just being dense- "did you kill all those raccoons?" or "who do you have buried in the crawlspace?" or, even better, "ewwww it's dead!" A lot of people saying this also eat fast food, buy meat at the grocery store, and let their cats roam outdoors…

I work humanely- in a sense. I don't kill anything to make my art but yes, they are real bones and skulls. I get them from a lot of different sources. Most of the game animal bones and skulls I get from hunters- I have friends who hunt for food, and who will give me remains to work with. Most of the deer, elk, and turkey skulls and bones I use come from these sources. I also get bones from family farms- chicken, pig, and goose or turkey bones, even a few ostrich and cow remains. Most of these animals are also killed for food.

I don't use anything from factory farms, just farms where the animals are treated well. I know this is enough to upset some people but since I also eat meat I don't feel bad about it- I WOULD feel awful using factory-farmed items. However if I came across some, or had a source, I might use them; that piece would probably be pretty damned dark though. I tend to work with the feelings the animal's remains give me, to make a piece that expresses the creature's life.

I know a lot of artists who work with animal remains are a bit more humorous than I am, or more light-hearted about it in general. I do see the remains as a medium but at the same time I don't feel good making jokes at the animal's expense. Very rarely I get a skull or part which is light, and happy- I will sometimes make a brighter piece with those. Usually though animals live difficult lives, and their bones speak to me about this, so I don't work very light very often.

I get questioned partly I think because of artists that do slaughter animals in the context of their work. While I don't do this, I don't find these artists offensive at all, it's just not my own way of working. I don't think it's horrible. I have hunted for food myself, and been present for slaughtering at farms. Again- I don't think it's awful if you eat at KFC, either. I just personally don't.

Some of my pieces come from road strikes. I have been working steadily on a series of photographs and an extended essay about roadside nature and roadkill, about human safety and how highways affect the animals that live near them. As a consequence of this work I have come across a LOT of roadside remains. I did get a license to collect roadkill in several states (not all states need one, but some do) and have spent a great deal of time working with these remains. A lot of these wild animals are obvious survivors of repeated injuries (fractures and old healed injuries in their skeletons attest to this) and the way they interact with the road fascinates me.

I have not used anything I myself ran over.

Most of my feathers come from friend's farms. Almost all of my plant matter comes from my own place- I live on the edge of the Siuslaw, and not only the yard/forest of my house but the clearcuts nearby furnish most of my lichens, moss, and wood. I do a lot of beach collecting too. I live in Oregon, and it is legal to collect many things here, since all beaches are public. I do refrain from collecting in park areas, since those are restricted. I also don't collect or mess with the remains of pinnipeds, or vertebrate fossils- just invertebrate fossils, collected in nonrestricted areas.

I have a few skulls and things which I have purchased. A few mink, fox, and beaver skulls which I am certain are fur trade castoffs- these items have a very dark feeling to them, and so the pieces built with them reflect that. I also have used vervet monkey skulls- the importation of these was a pain in the neck, and they are killed as a nuisance animal- so they too have a very dark feeling. Like I said, the horrors of life, death, the hard times most animals go through, are the reason my work is not light-hearted and silly. I don't use anything illegal, and I avoid using items which may violate CITES or the MBA. (More information on the legality of animal remains is available here, if you are interested.)

I don't work much with animals that are domestic pets, but I occasionally get some materials this way. Usually these are used for commissions for the previous owner. Some of these are more light and happy. I've worked with a very battered stray-dog skull, just making that piece was very upsetting. It wasn't a joke to me.

I've worked with human bones too. This is where people tend to be most alarmed- although in reality it is easier to buy human bone than many animals! I get most of my human bone specimens from places which sell vintage anatomical displays, or from places such as necromance (among others) which sell oddities. Yes, these bones are legal. No, I didn't kill anyone to get them. And YES, they are expensive for a reason. Again- most of these works are dark. I don't get silly feelings from death.

I've sold work and done commissions for vegans- for people who are animal and conservation activists. My work is intended to speak about the way people are oblivious to the natural world. Nature is full of drama, death, struggle, and strangeness. I try to use the materials I have to portray that. Reminders of mortality are not for everyone. Horrific art is not for everyone. There are people who cannot sit through a horror movie and people who cannot listen to a description of how their hamburger was made. My work is not for these people, really- although knowing that my work may have given them pause or made them think about these things, about the darker side of life, is kind of the point.

prints?

I always struggle with the question of whether to make downloads of my work available, or prints. In one way, I hate doing it, because I like the idea of something I made with my own hands going to your hands, as it is, with no other stuff there. Then I realize some things.

If I was a musician, I'd sell records, not just perform live.

I can only make so many original things, in so much time.

I'd like to be able to earn enough from my art to make it worth the time and energy (see footnote)

I have to eat.

Many people want to be able to enjoy my work but couldn't afford the cost of an original.

I can't manage shipping and storefronts online and promotion for all of that, and STILL HAVE TIME FOR MAKING THINGS.

I will take these point-by-point.

If I was a musician, I'd sell records. I'd want more people to enjoy my work than I could perform for in person. I'd want people to be able to take me anywhere with them. If I was a writer, I'd print books of my work. I wouldn't expect people to only access my work through attending readings, or by buying the hand-written manuscript. I'd want my work to be accessible, something people could enjoy. I also would maybe still sell the manuscript, or some signed first editions...but the books would be published, out there, even on a kindle.

I have two hands. If I work the equivalent of full-time hours, I can make maybe four things, of substandard quality, in a week. I can make maybe one or two things of good quality in a week. I can make one great thing a month. Now...how much is minimum wage? Should I set all the art aside and get a job at McDonald's? Because if I can only sell a piece of art one time, mcdonald's will pay better, and maybe I should set this art stuff aside permanently and get a real job...I can only make so much stuff with my own two hands. But if I sell prints and let people download the works, I can post it – set it and forget it. I can sell those while I am busy making other new things, and can continue to make money from a piece for years sometimes, long after the original is sold or destroyed.

I love making art. I spend all my time making things. I do have to eat. So therefore I have to charge money and sell my work– my choice is, work a job which takes all my time, and rarely make anything, or sell my work at a reasonable price and live off that money. I love making art. The process of actually making things, well, I will do that no matter what. I've had my Kafka years, working full-time then coming home and putting in another eight hours painting. But my work wasn't as good. And I had no time to show it to anyone. I need the time to show my work– to scan it, photograph it, share it, post it. If I don't make any money from a piece, I'll still MAKE the piece– but I will not spend the time posting it and discussing it and sharing it with you, or with anyone. If I was lucky enough to have inherited wealth maybe I'd have that kind of luxury, but I don't. I wish I did, really.

And yeah– YOU GUYS are broke too! I mean everyone is hurting. Being poor shouldn't mean you can't enjoy or own art! I want to make things accessible to everyone as much as possible. So– digital downloads. Most people have a printer– or access to a library with a printer in it– and can pay me a few dollars for a file, take it there, pay a buck or two to print it, and hang it up. Prints are next in line– the quality will be better, professional grade, the print will last longer, years even. Limited run? Why? It seems like a waste of time, of energy. I put my initials and a number on them and they're magically worth more somehow? No. I do handpainted prints though– the next higher price things– and those are fun. I can take an hour and embellish a painting I already did– make new details on it, play around. The buyer gets something unique, like an original, and I get to play…

I spend maybe an hour or two a day online writing copy for my work, explaining it, discussing it, sharing technical stuff, writing, posting, and keeping track of what has sold. I spend another hour or so every day taking photos, scanning, fixing the damn scanner. And another hour every other day packaging stuff to mail out, trying to keep track of what goes where. I am not good at any of these things. They are REAL WORK, hard work I don't enjoy very much. I'd rather be actually making things. So this work- I need to streamline it, make it as handsfree as possible. Selling originals is difficult. I have to post it everywhere, and hope the right person sees it, and then once it's sold, do it again, the entire process, from documenting the work to explaining it to answering questions and pricing it and packing it and shipping it. All that work has to be done completely from scratch, every time I sell an original.

A print? I scan it, touch it up, post it, and it's done. I can leave it there, just like that, for years. People can buy it a year later, without any additional work from me. It's what they call a secondary income stream, and as an artist working alone I NEED that to happen as much as possible. It frees up my hands for making more better things. The digital downloads are the same- even easier, in fact. There's no parameters to set, no material-checking, no worrying about quality control. It's set and forget.

So, in order to be able to make more and better art, and in order to live, I sell originals, downloads, AND prints of most things. I charge people a tiny bit extra if they buy an original and only want me to do a limited run of prints. I charge A LOT extra if someone buys something and wants me to make no prints at all...for example, A painting I make- the original is a hundred bucks. I will probably (if it's a good painting) make another two hundred off of prints and downloads of it over the course of a year. For me to sell ONLY THE ORIGINAL and still pay my rent, I have to charge three hundred for that original, now.

Should I do that? Sometimes I want to. Because I love the idea of something I made with my own hands, being in YOUR hands, with nothing in between us. Also because I like originals myself. But I can't manage to, or figure out how to, promote myself well enough to always sell my originals, let alone for three times what I have them priced at now. So unless a magical fairy of promotion comes and makes me famous or rich, without charging me anything or requiring more of my time to work it…I will keep selling prints and downloads, of nearly everything I make.

I love you guys. Those of you with two bucks, and those of you with a million. You're all people I like, and I want you all to be able to touch and enjoy my work.

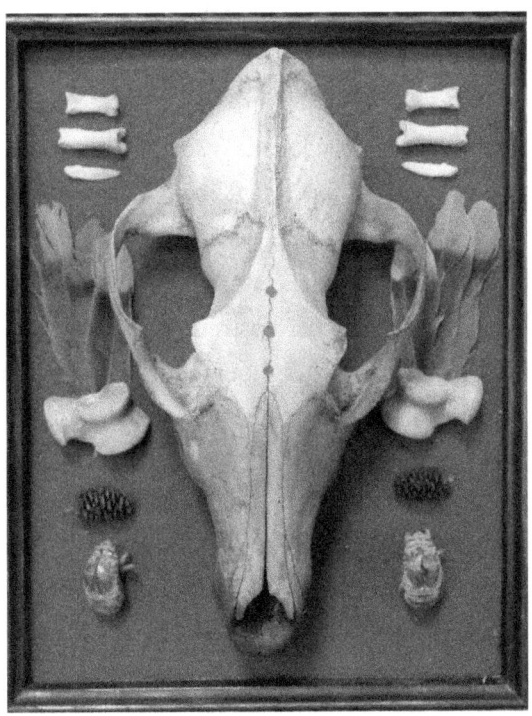

three lines.

I always use three lines/three dots on anything I do. Sometimes they're front and center, the focal point of the art, and Sometimes they're obscured- hidden in the backdrop or repeated in a pattern so as to be less noticeable.

I began doing this because of the greek character, Xi. There's a few layers of meaning there, and all of them combined made me interested in the symbol/shape, and that interest led to me using it as a part of my signature for a while. After that it migrated, getting further detached from my initials, and becoming more a part of the artwork. And from there it just sort of infiltrated every piece I make.

Back in the 80s-90s I was really interested in mindhacks and psychedelics and pTv and related art and music.

I did some work with sigils. I'm not a believer, not even agnostic, but I do know that our subconscious is a strong force, and that affecting it, changing it, tinkering in there, can bring some odd results. Working with visual symbols is one of my ongoing experiments- using an eye as the main focal point in a painting that is smaller and might be stolen from a gallery (even the most abstract eye affects the behavior of the people around it- see this study for details) or using hands, in various gestures, to suggest action to the viewer.

So while I have an abiding interest in all these things I am not any kind of believer. I do entertain the idea that Jung may have had a good point about how symbols and visual cues lead us, and have an impact on our lives, so it's always been my effort to find ways to incorporate these things, at least subtly, into my work. The three lines/dots is a personal symbol, though, which I use in my art to influence MYSELF. So in the sense of it meaning something to the viewer, maybe- it's done intentionally as a prompt to myself while working, though.

I like studying the I Ching, not for its woo-woo forcefield of prognostication, but for its base symbolism. The trigram ? in the I ching means, "the force of the small", power in a detail. Doubled, as a hexagram, it represents creativity.

Qian is the creative.The activity of qian is often fraught with tragedy (...), because humans with their finite vision embrace qian in lopsided ways, and their creative activity gets shunted into groupings.

This trigram represents transcendence. Going beyond, creating. Being uplifted. It has a really positive association for me, because of this.

..also the XI card in tarot is strength, or passion..

The old name for this card is "Fortitude". I think of it as stoicism in the pursuit of a passion; the ability to master forces opposing a goal. In the Crowley deck (gorgeous artwork!) this card is named "Lust", in the sense of great desire or passion in life. again- for me, these are really positive associations that can remind me, even if subconsciously, the drive and determination to finish a piece, to keep working even when things suck or are falling apart all around me- to keep pushing even when the art piles up and nobody wants it and my wrists hurt and I'm tired. It also reminds me to make my work as potent as possible.

=- is a letter of the greek alphabet.

In mathematics, it represents several things- the universal set (an all encompassing set of numbers/equations), implying wholism. Or, in chemistry, the extent of a reaction- the resonance of it.

It can be used to represent the number 60- making it the centerpiece of a sort-of-moronic controversy about the number 666, of which it's the central character.

It's also used, turned to its side, as a symbol for conditional equality in an equation. In other words, the answer will hold true in that case but may not hold true in others. as in $X=a*b$

There's an uncertainty about it.

Then, there's the lines and dots together. First of all, I call them sweat lines, because they remind me of the way cartoonists draw sweat popping off of a character who's in trouble. But they also are a druid symbol, related to inspiration. Since, again, I am not religious at all, the whole "food of the gods" story here doesn't mean much- but the idea that inspiration can appear from outside the self, and be disseminated then by the things you create with that...I can get my hooks into that.

Three dots is an ellipsis, implying that there is more to come, that the thought is unfinished...

I have a tiny tattoo on my hand of three dots. Yep, it's a 'Mi Vidi Loca' tattoo. Yes, my life has been crazy. I tend to draw from all that weird experience in the things I make and do.

There's more to it too, I have a bit of a compulsion to do things in sets of three in general. So even when I use the three lines/dots as a background pattern, they'll appear in multiples of three throughout the piece. But all that's a story for another day.

INTERNETS

resonant.

I was very interested in physics. Always have been. I found the concept of resonance fascinating, and still do. Not just in its technical aspect but also in its more esoteric forms, and as a metaphor for how I create things and where my ideas come from. And I thought hard about a username. After all, this was my first email account.

Resonance is a state in which things move in a particular rhythm. The basic thought is that when something is struck with a force that matches its own innate, natural rhythm, it will start to move in sympathy- resonate.

If you play the right note next to a tuning fork, it will vibrate.

This is of course just the basic scientific idea of resonance. But I'm a fan of using half-assed metaphors from scientific thought to explain other things in life. When I was younger I had done a lot of reading; notably in this case reading Jung, Tesla, and Sheldrake.

Sheldrake's theory of morphic resonance is pretty interesting, even if not proven. That living things should always follow their predecessors in shape due to a repeated preference in evolution for that particular design is a simple enough thought. But proposing that unrelated creatures would also influence each other is a bit more of a leap. I find it interesting, though, and would love to see some work done to test the idea further.

Tesla's work with resonance is purely done from a physics perspective, but has its implications.

Jung, of course, talks a lot about the collective unconscious. Now taking into account the other things I just brought up, you can see where I'm heading. If everything has its own natural rhythm, its own note, then why would the human mind be any different?

As the world around us changes, as events occur, the hive mind begins to shiver. Every worker bee shakes its ass to the same beat. (with exceptions- although I've always found some pride in being a rebel)

I always felt like somehow the things I saw with my mind's eye were just reactions to the world around me, reactions that I didn't control. I have always been a fan of the surrealists. How do you paint a dream? And does what we make, as art, come from some inner vision? How do you represent the impossible, visually? How do we make a picture of the mystery?

Everything I make is a product of the world's rhythm, and the things that strike me in just the right way, with just the right amount of force, and with the proper chord, will resonate. I will move, and what my eye invents will come out through my hands and into the world. Like a note from a tuning fork. I don't act in rhythm with the world- only when it hits me just right, do I resonate. Only the things with which I resonate, do I respond to this way.

I don't think that I can explain much more clearly than that. I actually did think about all this when I picked that name; at the time I thought it would be a short-lived name, but it has stuck for more than fifteen years and I don't think I'll be changing it any time soon.

Especially in tattooing, I work with the zeitgeist. I see trends. I can almost, if I squint just right in low light, see the future. Art shows us where we are going, where we are, what we've been. Art is the Cassandra of civilization. We see the consequences, and without trying to propagandize even, we express the effects of change in the world through what we make. My hand can draw the future out on a piece of paper, and I can sell a thousand copies. But whether or not people pay attention to art as an indicator of our coming dystopia is another question, one I don't have an answer to, one I haven't finished wrestling with yet.

etsy.

The place has always had resellers; people breaking the rules to pass off mass-produced stuff as handmade.

There's a lot of money to be had from people who want to NOT support corporations, who want to buy local, handmade stuff. A lot of people don't like buying things that were made for pennies by slave labor. Lots of companies know that, and will lie about how their stuff was made, to get that dollar.

The people who produce things with slave labor want that dollar, too.

"Former eBay and PayPal executive Stephanie Tilenius has joined the Board of Directors of Etsy, joining Etsy founder Rob Kalin, FlickR's Caterina Fake, Union Square Ventures' Fred Wilson, and Accel Partners' Jim Breyer (also on Walmart.com.'s board) on the board. Tilenius left eBay last year and now heads Google's commerce division."

So they invaded etsy (and a few other places) and have been trying for a while now to find ways to successfully sell to people who don't want to buy from them. Recently, an attempt to pass off furniture built in Bali as "handmade in CA" was busted. The thing is- etsy isn't supposed to be a place to buy factory-made goods being resold. Its own mission statement says that buying direct from people who are making things by hand, not in factories, is the point.

I signed up there because of that but now...well, the fact that when confronted with a (GIANT SHITPILE OF) evidence, including an email from the man who actually makes the furniture, that the stuff is not produced in CA, and that the original seller is a fraud, etsy chose not to apologize, not to admit fault and remove the seller—but to close discussions about it and deny. (note- the fraudulent seller? is not only still open, but still in their list of "featured sellers")

So, I'm in the process of migrating. (check out my home page- new links to my stuff for now! All my rocks, sticks, logs, and moss will stay on etsy- but anything I made, art, paintings and stuff- originals- has been moved. still debating whether to keep my prints there or not, my "production work")

A lot of other artists and craftsmen warned me about etsy but- the traffic! People I didn't already know were able to find my work there. I like that! I want people to see my art, and buy it, so I can pay rent and things like that. But then I started thinking about it harder.

have you ever played the game "Go"? there's a saying in that game, don't throw good stones after bad. like once it's obvious your grouping will be captured, don't continue to add more stones to it, because those will be captured too...like, if something will eat all the resources you give it STOP NOW no matter how much you've already invested.

here's the forum post I made in a private thread over there:

I'm a sensitive artist-person. I'm the twee, woods-living, eccentric painter with thoreau and van gogh all up in my brain. I am a commie, a lefty pinko. I am what etsy pretends to be. I actually am that stuff.

I am sometimes unstable and I have to fight and struggle really hard to be productive, to be prolific. My life is hard work. I have arranged my life now to avoid things which throw me off, which offend my internal sense-o-meter.

I haven't watched shows on a TV in almost a decade (I watch one or two here and there online). I don't listen to commercial radio. I don't shop in malls, in large corporations. I haven't in years. I just can't, I am too goddamn sensitive to the ramifications of it to stand it.

I signed up on etsy because I bought their schtick. I am suddenly sad thinking about the people I have introduced to this place, being called dunces, being lied to.

I mean, it's MY integrity at stake here. It's MY word that people should come to etsy- every time I link to my stuff here I am sending my own friends and family's dollar and eyes into it.

I am disturbed by all this. I knew this kind of thing was happening here but the lack of public apology and that the situation has been handled this way upsets me. I think that my decision to stay on etsy, when I was prepared to leave before, may be the reason I have had artist's block off and on. I think that for someone like me it is unbearable, and it kills my muse, to be associated with this kinda stuff.

The ocean actually does fucking talk to me. I know it's cheeseball BUT, all that marketing crap is stolen from the words of people who do actually have that kind of creative impetus. That's a real way of living- the same way there are hoboes hopping trains right now, with toothaches and no work to be had- there are some of us who hole up and just CREATE, and who feel the tides and smell the moon and stuff.

So yeah, I guess tl,dr: I don't know if I can handle being associated with this kind of lack-of-integrity stuff just for my own mental health- and my clients and friends! fuck- you guys TRUST ME not to send you to some asshole to buy something shitty. Why would I do that? I don't want you to stop trusting my recommendations of places and things. I only tell you about things I like! fuck that...also- I'm a tattoo artist, I don't HAVE TO put up with bullshit.

I used to be a crusty punk WAY back when. I remember when I first saw someone with a mohawk playing "punk rock" on mtv, and thinking to myself- they won't keep the truth of it, the reason for it. they're going to sell the goddamn haircut but not the POINT OF what we were trying so hard to gain-

the politics of it, the basic respect for humanity, the blistered hands from learning to build things, the DIY ethic...all gone in a flash, turned into crappy plastic boots that fall apart in a year...

but here I am, living out my idealistic teenage dreams, making things with my own two hands. so punks not dead. DIY will live forever, people making things themselves, and selling or sharing art and craft doesn't end just because etsy sucks. no- it's just another website dying, playing its swansong while public opinion decrees it uninteresting. and since I was making stuff before the internet even existed-

internet and art.

Putting your art up online is kind of like showing it in a gallery. You may not be the best at your particular art style, but if you want to improve, showing the internet what you are doing is a good way to get better. There are so many skill levels, so many ways of expressing yourself; the internet is home to them all.

If you're really timid, start slow. Use deviantart, and request critiques. Once you feel like you can handle more harsh views, try some art forums, and ask for opinions.

Or, alternately, you can dive right in. We all start where we are. Try to get very good pictures of your work. never upload giant files; upload files that are just big enough to look good on a monitor, no larger. Image theft is common, and sometimes unintentional. If you watermark unobtrusively, and only upload smaller files, you'll find more people credit you when reposting or sharing your work. You want people to do that, because that is how you will sell your art online.

Etsy is a good starter for artists. It's not the best venue for fine art, but it can be a good way to get your feet wet. Be cautious, though, as most of the advice on using etsy is not written with art in mind, but easily-reproducible craft. Your painting can't be tagged and posted the same way a t-shirt can. This is why etsy is only a starter site.

You could also opt for one of the other sites geared for art sales- originals are harder to sell most places than prints, but it IS possible to sell just originals online. Squareup.com.market, nd zibbet.com are better alternatives than etsy for most things.

If you are just starting out, keep your prices as low as possible. Once you are selling your work on a regular basis, then you can raise your prices. At first, it's unknown if you will succeed or not. Most people not only buy art for its look, for how it grabs the eye, but also for the artist's longevity, their name, their history. Build your history a little!

It's the internet. You should maintain privacy for your own comfort and safety of course-but letting people get to know you, talking about deep or personal things, lets the viewer understand the origin of your works, and become more invested in them. Give them a chance to find out where the art came from. You can be a cantankerous bitch hermit like me and STILL be capable of showing your inner self online. You don't have to be outgoing to do it; you can talk as if the site was your own art journal, your own notes about each piece.

So- yeah. Your art is good enough to sell online- at etsy or anywhere else. Keep your expectations of sales low at first, and your prices the same, and then as time passes you will see how your work can fit into the greater whole of online art.

And if you need encouragement, ask for it. And if you need a slap on the wrist, or a sound drubbing, you should ask for that too. All the help you could ever want from other artists lives inside your computer, but it can only do you good if you put your own work in there too.

WATERMARKS.

I've seen my work posted and reposted a lot online (it probably started in earnest, with my work, when a large tree tattoo I'd done was the main image on the wikipedia "tattoo" entry for almost a year) and I've never really thought about the amount of people who may be seeing it with no idea who made it.

A few things recently made me consider starting to watermark my stuff with my site's address. First, I was looking at sketches done by some artists on a social network site I use, and found a sketch of my spider monkey mount's skull and jaws. It was a great sketch, and I commented on it saying I loved that someone was using my work as inspiration. The artist blew it off, saying "Yes, I found this randomly online." They had no idea they were talking to the creator of the work they were (tracing) drawing.

I explained that it was my work, she was excited to find out where it came from, we made friends.

It was a really good sketch.

Then, I found my spider skeletons posted to a russian site- and have no idea what on earth it says, whether it links back to me (update- it does) or not, and would love to comment but have no idea which buttons are for commenting or anything since I don't read cyrilic.

Should I start watermarking things? I'd love it if every time my work was reposted or re-used, someone new came to see the rest of what I do, came here and maybe even said hi or spoke with me.

Having the site address on each photo is something I have alternately been too obstinate, or too lazy, to do. I don't think even if I did this, that I would have the patience to go back and watermark all my older images (about twenty thousand images of my various works exist online) but maybe, going forward, I should make the effort.

Keep your mouth shut, eat money.

I'm pretty vocal about politics. I've been told by a lot of my regular collectors that they like this- while they may disagree with me on certain issues, they also appreciate knowing where my head is at, and find my rants either amusing or rousing, depending on their own stance.

I was recently talking to another artist I know, though, who said that he keeps his opinions to only his personal circle, because he's afraid that the people who buy his work might stop buying it if he speaks his mind.

Now, this guy doesn't hold any really fringe ideas, like I do sometimes. He's a lot more centrist than me, his opinions are not really all that strange. I mean to say, he's not like politically supporting puppy-kicking as a national sport, or anything outlandish like that. Nothing unusual enough to put him at too much risk of heavily alienating most people, I'd think.

His worry, and I quote, is that "because I want health coverage, I think the richer people who collect my work will think I'm some kind of welfare leech, those people think that way. If I spoke my mind, some of them would find out I despise them and think they're the leeches, that their politics are the politics of greed and I don't want to go broke because a few rich people want to not have to pay taxes, and get angry when I say I think they should". He was really upset about this subject, because he's working with a cause group for an issue and feels like he can't talk openly about those efforts. And it's a cause he really believes in, so he feels like he can't support it publicly...which sucks.

Man, am I ever lucky that most of my collectors are people who don't earn a billion a year. I used to get envy for this guy- I mean, he makes a really good living, he can afford a nice car and a visit to the dentist and a hundred other things out of my price range, all from selling his art. But! the price is his integrity, in a way. He has to kiss ass. He has to keep his dirty prole mouth shut, in order to pay rent on that big studio.

I kind of feel bad for him. But at the same time, I understand. I've said a lot of things very publicly that I'm sure have turned some people away from my work, whether it's my support for abortion rights, access to health care for all, my hatred for landlords, or that I like volvos...if someone wants a reason not to buy some art, they'll find one.

I blame my own openness on my previous involvement with groups like QN/ACTUP, and AYF, among others, back in my younger years. Silence=death, truer words were never shouted out loud. I learned from my early political growth that speaking your mind is important to the world, that keeping quiet allowed bad things to continue and that being outspoken was almost something you owed the world...

If someone is moved by something they will buy it- they'll almost HAVE to buy it. The reasons not to buy will not even get found, discussed, or considered. I could be really wrong about this, but I think most people who buy art (except for "investing in art" type people... who only care about your notoriety) are buying art that speaks to them, not supporting some cause, or looking for politics, or whatever. They just like the art. The artist is only important to them in the sense of backstory for something they want to look at often- we're only the maker. We're not and shouldn't be, the selling point.

But then again conventional wisdom is that artists need to have some kind of shiny personality or quirkiness and "sell themselves" and show up at opening to glad-hand everyone. If that was an indicator of good art, Ron Popeil would be a better artist than Van Gogh (who was fairly anti-social, actually).

People like me who are a bit less interested in the social aspects of selling art, or people like my friend who are crushed by that, have a really hard time sometimes. It's one of the reasons I have turned down the few "actual gallery" offers I've gotten. I don't want to change who I am, live in town, go out and drink wine and talk in a crowded room. I just don't. I show in bars, in little galleries (like the Unfine Art Museum) that allow me the freedom of being an asshole if I want to be.

I mean, I'd love to have the exposure and funds my friend has, but not at the price he's paying for it, if you know what I mean.

Now, with tattooing, I'll argue the whole time I work on someone. Hearty debates make the time pass, and it seems like they distract people from the pain of the tattoo time, which is a good thing. I have tons of tattoo clientele who disagree with me really vocally and intensely on things, and some of those conversations are the ones I treasure, and remember for a long time after. In tattooing it's less of an impediment I think. The connection you get with people you've tattooed is totally different than the one people get by buying some art for the wall. It's a lot more alive, more intense and personal. For me, it's a really good contrast to the way the art world seems to be- there's no question of manners and politeness and being "nice": just loud, blunt, openness.

It's a good thing for me to have in my life. I think being that open, for me, has been more an advantage than a drawback. For my friend, maybe he just needs to find collectors that agree with him. Who knows? I don't.

self-promotion.

Promotion comes easily to a lot of tattooers. When I first started tattooing, I was shy, a hermit. I disliked talking to people and pretty much felt uncomfortable in my own skin. I did not, and do not now, have great social skills and an outgoing personality. I also have always been a geek, nerd, dork. A skank. A weirdo. Not popular.

Promotion requires friendliness. You have to like people, to convince them that there is good reason for them to come to you for their visual needs. Yes, skill and talent and innate genius go a long way, but not all the way. You have to learn to shake hands and smile. To play nice.

I discovered, after tattooing for a few years, that I genuinely liked the people I was working on. Tattoo clientele vary regionally of course, but

I found that even the "worst" client base were people that I naturally thought were pretty cool. They wanted to get a tattoo. Often they were witty, or silly, or just interesting. I decided I liked these people.

And I discovered that I liked tattoo artists a whole lot too. They understood me- and usually, they were in the same sort of dilemma I was- not the "cool kids" until after they'd started to get better at this job. So we were all struggling in some way, to be social at work. There are exceptions to this of course but I feel that they are rare. We did not fit in, in some way, which is why we chose this field.

You have to realize that nobody cares. Put simply, nobody at all cares about you, your art, your struggles- no matter how famous you become or how rich, no matter how talented- in the end, nobody cares. Your job when promoting is to MAKE THEM care.

Being friendly with clientele while still being professional is difficult. There's a line there that you do not want to cross. But if you are genuinely interested in your clients and in your co-workers, and you respect them and express interest and support, you will find much more of the same in return.

It sounds ridiculous to say, but give everybody your business cards. Yes, even your mom. Yes, even the yoga teacher that your daughter goes to at the Y. Everybody, no holds barred. You should be the tattoo artist in their lives. Everyone you meet or know, at some point, should consider you their "tattoo friend".

Giving other artists your card pays off too, because the things you can learn over a glass of whiskey at four AM cannot be summarized in print.

WILD THEORIES

general strike.

I think we should do it.

If you're democrat, go on general strike because the government is planning to use poor people's money to finance rich people's bailout. Plus, we could have our universal health care and better schools for that ticket price. It's a colossal waste, and it's corrupt, and you guys are so totally against that.

If you're republican, go on general strike because they're killing the free market. By bailing out failing businesses and banks, we're destroying our nation's last grasp at real capitalism. We're financing the weak! We're making a bad investment, sending good money after bad...you should be even more infuriated than the left wing. I don't know why you're not- don't you like the free market? Do you want the government to own everything? Do you like the idea that the government pays for businesses that are incapable of supporting themselves?

Let's have a general strike, on monday. Everyone take the day off. Fuck it.

If they don't listen to that, we've got nothing left but wholescale revolution (and I for one am not in the mood right now)

the muppet movie

The Muppet Movie (the original one) was made by Henson as a morality tale for people working in creative fields, reminding them to help newcomers.

The movie is self-referential, and has three recursive layers, all stating the same theme.

Henson is simultaneously 1.asking for help to attain his dreams, 2. encouraging the muppets to attain their dreams, and 3. offering help and encouragement to the audience, to attain their own.

The theme song, Rainbow Connection, says as much, metaphorically- Creatives are represented throughout the movie by rainbows. There are so many songs about rainbows because rainbows make all the songs!

The entire movie is a discussion about creativity, and its place in the world, and how to overcome things in order to succeed with a creative mind. Finding friends who will support you- this is not only shown by the kindliness of the muppets to new passengers, but in a meta sense by the human cast of the movie, many of whom worked on it for very low pay.

When they help other creative creatures they have very good luck- kermit helping fozzie bear, for example, gets him a ride and a companion who can drive. when they arrive at the church, the band helps them by camoflaging their car, and letting them get a glimpse at the script. There is no fourth wall to be broken, it's wide-open through to the audience the entire time.

when they don't help others, they fail at their goals- when miss piggy leaves kermit to go see her agent, she doesn't get the part. after this, when they are in the desert, gonzo sings about the longing for a settled life, and knowing that, as a creative type, he can never attain that, can never go back to living normally.

The corporate/business-minded people, like the villianous frog-leg restaurant owner, want to profit from the creative creatures, want to quantify the rainbow- and that can't be done.

At the end of the movie, when they arrive at the studio, they are allowed in immediately to pitch their movie idea (the journey they just now took) and are instantly given a contract. This is another layer of "creative workers are ethically obligated to help others who are just starting out"- rainbows helping and encouraging rainbows.

Then, the movie as a whole, is a message of kindness, encouragement, and welcome to new artists and creative people, telling them that their imagination is welcome and needed, and that they are part of that family, that rainbow tribe.

It was made to show younger viewers that older artists WOULD help and teach them, and give them opportunity; also, it was made to show adult artists that the best and most vital use of fame and money is the kindling of talent in the newcomers, those who show up with an idea and nothing else in their wallets.

Rainbows connect, rainbows are only half of a circle. Put two rainbows end-to-end, and you have this movie. A movie about some people getting their movie made, with some help from movie makers- and a song about rainbows, sung, and written, by a rainbow.

pleasures.

To discuss my personal beliefs is incredibly difficult.

It is so much easier to review and criticize external stimuli, than it is to describe the meanderings of the internal stimuli. That said, I think I am a (quasi-)liberal (meta-)secular (post-)humanist, of sorts.

I believe that there are many, infinitely many, universes, and that because of this there are infinitely many possibilities. Therefore, I shyly believe that my own mind is a wee holographic chunk of the whole, reflecting it, and therefore, I also believe my mind is pretty.

Since there are infinite possibilities, it becomes clear that I will probably live forever. Not possibly, but probably. This sounds very strange but is backed up somewhat concretely by recent thinking and research into quantum physics and chaos theory mathematics. New advances in medicine make it more likely that my stay on this particular small pinpoint we call earth will be long and exhausting.

Now, before any burning-man hippy types begin to think they are more exhaustively well-read than I am on generally trippy concepts, I am indeed already aware that anyone who has read even a few chapters of "food of the gods", "timewave zero", or any other light or heavy work by terence and Dennis Mckenna has some arguments waiting for me at the end of this paragraph.

Allow my rebuttal.

While quantum mechanics and higher math are,indeed, simply another faith-based cosmology, they do have a high level of verifiability in reality. Two apples added to two apples is, indeed, four apples. (or four apples worth of apple sauce, if you are some kind of topography geek.) Mathematics, even in its highest and most impenetrable forms, can be proven step at a time in tangible sense. Physics also has a high level of credibility, even though on a molecular and particular level it becomes difficult to observe real effects. Therefore, even though math and science are simply a new 21st century religion, they are also more credible than this...or even this. Until evidence changes the results of current research(change...yet another reason science is more credible than older religions) I will take these conclusions in part or whole and warp them to suit myself, all I like. Remember, we're talking about my internal stimuli.

Although I welcome conclusion-shattering arguments, too. They're actually how I ended up where I am now.

Granted all of these things boiling in my head, and you can see how the next logical question becomes;"what to do to keep from getting bored?"

With infinite eons stretching out ahead, and the limited antics and amusements legally available to me here, the only downfall it that for at least the foreseeable several centuries will see me contained in this somewhat defective body, which unfortunately came equipped with substandard strength, height, and flexibility, and has acquired over time a somewhat cluttered paint job, along with hairy moles and aching joints.

I am in favor of any technology, of any sort, which will make it possible for me to ;

wear giant biomechanical grasshopper legs and leap into the stratosphere,

change my fullbody tattoo daily, even make it invisible if I want... (actually, I'm working on that one with some help from a secret science-type friend right now)

talk to my friends through a cochlear ear implant that picks up sound osteologically and transmits it via bluetooth to the implants in their teeth,

see in the dark,

communicate with animals,

have sex for days at a time without tiring or drying out,

and trip face. totally. trip face.

Thinking about all of this makes me feel a whole lot better about the fact that change is constant and somewhat terrifying. That aging, death, disease, illness, loneliness, physical and intellectual pain....that all of that is here too.

I'm not a luddite, I also really have no respect for most belief systems that logically (or irrationally) progress to thinking that life is suffering, (byebye buddha and st paul), that some people are more entitled to opportunity than others because of irrelevancies like age, sex, faith,or color,-entitled to opportunity,I say, not the ability to take it-(bye bye st peter, hitler, jesus, mohammed, ghandi, MLK, malcolm x, GWB,YHWH,Dworkin,etc....well, all of them, really.),nor do I much appreciate the notion that humankind is here to work and must do so or be damned, or that life is agony, or any of that crap.

I've had some very hard times in my life. They are not what I'm here for. They are merely the bit of shadow that makes the light seem brighter. That is their only purpose.

And so we come full circle to my vice of pronoia. I indulge in this constantly. Even at the darkest part of my mind, glimmers this notion that somehow the universe will pull me through. It is truly a vice, too. In the classical sense. It tastes like candy, it smells like fucking, it sounds like punk rock and it looks like a fat glass of whiskey with no hangover attached.

It feels good.

It makes sense.

I mean, why would I want fun, if that's not the whole point? I can hardly wrap my mind around the extent of divine cruelty if there was some sort of deity making us all want pleasure, but requiring us to experience pain...and then punishing us for the wanting. It makes no sense at all unless you truly believe your god is pretty much the devil. And that's ridiculous. (sorry,guys.)

So...it's just that infinity exists in a vacuum. and that makes everything possible, pleasant and not-so-pleasant. There are ways to avoid the unpleasantnesses of this world, and I know of a few reliable ones I can share...

1.Get born in the First world, preferably northern Europe;

2.Be white,

3.Get or find or inherit material wealth,without caring too much about it;

4.Eat,drink,taste,try,fuck,and dance to every single thing you possibly can.

I am not trying to say that everything is sweetness and light all the time, or that grief and fear have no place...just that I indulge myself in thinking there is a light at the end of the tunnel, and that the tunnel itself is long, windy, fascinating, and full of hilarity in its own right.

Human evolution has not stopped. Our bodies and minds have continued to evolve to respond to new environments...The increase in rate of autism is a prime example. If you have Asperger's syndrome, you may (it is now thought) be the next step in human physical and mental evolution. Apparently the future is rife with non-social interactions, making emotional interference in life's more meaningful concerns a recidivist throwback to the apes, or something like that. Robots are our friends!

We are more and more spending our time as a species(in more tech-savvy nations, anyway...Swaziland is probably not spawning a lot of autistics) dealing with technology, remote communications, and intellectually stimulating culture. Despite some pop-culture trends, sentimentality is only prevalent in some backwards areas of the developed world. Low emotional affect has become more prevalent with each generation. It's another mental vice for me-thinking that the human mind of the future is more like my own.

For everyone else, it may help to realize that if we seize the reins of evolution firmly, we can shape ourselves into anything we want. Nanotech and stem cells and the human genome project and cloning... the 21st century lives up to every mad scientist's fondest dreams. Evolution is not some force, like a deity, that will get angry or jealous if we overcome it and steer it. Evolution is simply a rule which can be countered and understood. Unlike a deity it should not be anthropomorphized. It has no vengeance.

I'm not saying that bird flu isn't scary. Just that it's not mother nature" "having a snit". It's just another organism flowing down the morphological hill into the future, like we still are. As soon as we control our physical destiny, we will be different from other life forms. Sentience, by itself, does not make us any different. We're simply a higher degree on a continuum.(I am an omnivore, by the way. Life feeds on death. And all that malarkey.)

Altering our biology the way we are soon going to able to-that, that is another story.

Maybe this alteration, this tinkering, is the singularity many scientists think we are approaching. Maybe it will be some kind of change in consciousness, instead. Or maybe we will all just die out from some mega-plague or monster asteroid or alien invasion...zombies, tidal waves, what-have-you. But maybe it will be that we change so fundamentally the way we are in the universe, that we become unrecognizable...

Money frees you from doing things you dislike. Since I dislike doing nearly everything, money is handy. Groucho Marx

How nice—to feel nothing, and still get full credit for being alive. Kurt Vonnegut,

To acquire knowledge, one must study; but to acquire wisdom, one must observe. Marilyn vos Savant

Early to rise and early to bed makes a male healthy and wealthy and dead. James Thurber

The point of philosophy is to start with something so simple as not to seem worth stating, and to end with something so paradoxical that no one will believe it. Bertrand Russell

"We shouldn't fear a world that is more interacted." –George W. Bush, Washington, D.C., June 27, 2006

hypnotizing people so they'll like you.

When I read these "hinty" how-to websites they make my blood run cold. I am NOT a deer in the headlights! Women are NOT thinking "my, how suave he is! I am dazed by his firm touch and for some reason I feel COMPELLED to fuck him, I wonder why?"

Subliminal messages don't work this way. What she is thinking is "Oh man that was somehow really revolting, but I can't quite put my finger on exactly WHY that guy makes me want to vomit. Let go of me you FREAK!"

I have had guys do this kind of stuff and I swear it is just repellent. There's this one guy that I talked to one night, he seemed normal and cool enough, not unattractive, and he asked me if I wanted to go play pool with him sometime. I said OK, we'll maybe try to do that, but then when he said goodnight he touched my lower back, just brushy like it was an accident. O man I almost hurled on him. I felt like someone had rubbed shit on me. It was just so....creepy! Creepy! EEEWWW!!! Don't fucking touch people! Were you absent the day in kindergarten when they explained "personal space"? Like, a handshake is sensible. A handshake is friendly. A smile is nice. But reaching lightly for my ass LIKE I DIDN'T NOTICE IT??? I am NOT blind or senseless! I can tell you are creepy! I CAN TELL!!!

It was supposed to, I presume, make me think of having his hands elsewhere-which I immediately decided was no longer interesting. Gross. I spoke to the guy a few weeks later and he told me it was a "technique" (his word) he'd learned from some website. How horrific. He was doing fine until he tried to mesmerize me. What, this poor guy can only get a date by swinging a watch at a girl and intoning "you are sleeeepy" in some sepulchral voice, while his eyes are all marty-feldman-swirly-crazed? It's freaking ridiculous and it is a turn off...

Like, a handshake is sensible. A handshake is friendly. A smile is nice. But A pause, and then some kind of "trying to be intense" moment during a handshake? WHAT THE FUCK? Let go you FREAK! Don't touch people in places they haven't offered for you! Don't try to hide what you are after, or try to make them ask you for something YOU want...

spineless cowards! Shifty, no-honor, unchivalrous, lying leeches! It is just unattractive!

It's so much better to se the guy take a risk, you know, rather than subliminally trying to implant the notion that they are "charming" into your head when you are not looking. what, you don't know how to talk to people ? You have NO social skills at all? I have had men that were terrified of women, truly, do better than this just by saying "I am scared but I like you. " How much cooler is THAT????

It implies that any woman in their right mind will not "put out" unless they are first hypnotized. Why not just get yourself a tranquilizer gun and just shoot them so they'll like you? Isn't that easier than BEING someone women would like? Gawd! Fuck!

nihilism.

I am an atheist. Well, technically, I am a nihilist.

Atheists tend to believe in the good nature of humanity, or the ability to make the world a better place, or willpower, or some such like. A lot of them enjoy viewing the Universe as a remarkable place full of wonder.

A lot of them want to build community, work together to improve life for everyone. Many are generous and kind, and think that empowerment of others is a good thing. Most atheists are dedicated to making this world, the only world they believe in, a better place in general.

I like atheists. I like them a lot. You can tell that a lot of them are optimistic about humanity's chance to survive, about our ability as human beings to turn around the destructive forces within us. Forces like hate, religion, patriotism, racism. Most atheists I know want some kind of peace, some way to make it easier for human beings to work together.

They also are very curious about the way the world functions, about the mechanics and the meaning of it all, in ways that religious people simply are not. Religions answer all the questions, without giving any explanation, and to question is heresy. For atheists, questioning and finding explanations is the purpose.

Did I say I like atheists? Because I really, really like them.

Anyway, I'm a bit more of a nihilist. I think the human race, as a species, is doomed to certain extinction, and sooner rather than later. I think that it's already far too late to do anything like make vasectomies and abortion mandatory and oil and fossil fuels illegal; I think we have passed the window in which such drastic measures would have saved us. We've pretty much shitted this place up beyond repair.

The world will go on. The earth and whatever animals and plants manage to evolve to suit the coming changes. Humanity, on the other hand, I do not think will persevere. We haven't destroyed the planet, only our own chances of surviving on it. If perhaps we'd been able to overcome our lizard-brains long enough to stop breeding and greeding, we might have staved it off.

But now- with the top tiny number of humans in control of almost all resources, and the rest frothing at the bit to revolt- it is likely too late for turning back.

I may be an old woman when this happens, or I may not live to see it. Or it could begin now, tomorrow, tonight. I have no way of knowing. But I will, as all humans do, live out my life. If that means a grim aeon in a cage or cell, so be it. If it means eating soylent green, ok then. If it means starving or being shot, well that's what happens to some humans, right?

We're all doomed to die. It's a certainty. And we're doomed to die OUT, as well.

People who are breeding, driving massive SUVs, cutting forests, and the like- well, technically that's evil. If I believed in such a thing. What was once the highest purpose for most people- hoarding and breeding-is now the worst imaginable modern demon. Greed and narcissistic reproduction have been allowed to flourish until- now- we are all doomed.

All of this is not to say that I do not enjoy my life. My life is all there is, and right now, it's enjoyable. I will always want to know what happens next, even if my doomsaying nature thinks it can't possibly be anything good.

Also, it's fun to watch atheists try. They would give me hope, if I believed in such a thing.

And yes I know- I'm not supposed to talk about what I really think or believe. I'm supposed to be mute, or at the very least neutral, or else nobody will want to buy my art.

I'm sorry- but Picasso was an avowed womanizer and plenty of conventionally-moral women hung his works in their home. Van Gogh publicly adored hookers, and now the middle class has bunches of sunflowers in their front rooms.

I feel that if someone likes my art, they like my art, and will buy it. If they don't personally like me, it shouldn't matter- it adds strength to the story behind the piece, actually. ("I got it from this eccentric crazypants") And if people disagree with me, I suppose I will just starve, as most vocal artists tend to do.

It's our punishment, you see. Society likes to watch us frustrated, poor, and suffering. They don't like their artists rich, fat, and happy- they save that for people whose skill is in manipulating others, owning cheap labor. and moving it from place to place.

on beauty.

Beauty, as a subjective term, is all around us. Or, beauty is rare, fleeting, and often hidden. While we can apply some objective standards to certain objects, others are ineffable.

The human eye responds strongly with a positive reaction to curves more than straight lines, and to S-curves more than single curves. Our eyes' receptor cells are actually soothed by subdued blue tones, and inflamed by bright reds and oranges.

We'll usually think something is beautiful if it is balanced or symmetrical, and if it speaks to us emotionally. However, although objects that have grace and depth are beautiful according to many sources, others find schmaltzy greeting cards or stark gray buildings beautiful.

Why such conflict in taste? If our eyes are all set up with the same cells, what is it that makes our perceptions so different?

Partly, it is our culture. In western countries, wearing eighteen or nineteen large copper rings to elongate one's neck would not be considered beautiful, but in some places on earth it's the epitome of style. Art, clothing, architecture, and personal adornments are incredibly diverse on this earth, and our heritage plays a large part in our aesthetic tastes. Someone who was raised to enjoy clean air and sunshine will not understand the appeal of even the most austere and graceful skyscraper, and someone who was raised in stately brownstones will not see the beauty in an elegantly carved mosque. These are basic differences in background, though, and people in the same culture also disagree. Why?

Partly, it's lifestyle. A rich society matron may think that a yellow diamond is gorgeous, while a trainyard worker may see more beauty in a glimmering star at sunset. We find beauty in the things we are exposed to, in order to find value in our own world. We look around, and we compare things in our environment, and we decide what we like to look at. The things we find beautiful are things we can encounter in our own life, and that gives us great satisfaction even if they are fleeting. But still, two people living in the same place with the same lifestyle can have completely opposite tastes. What happened?

They had different experiences. No matter how alike we are to someone, even if we are conjoined twins, we experience things from a different perspective than anyone else on earth. We see things from only our own eyes, from our own viewpoint. Someone who hates children may not find a baby beautiful, but someone who loves them will melt. This is the emotional component of aesthetic taste. If we are emotionally attached to someone, it does not matter what they look like; we will see a glow around them. Our emotions alter our perceptions more than many of us would like to admit- even the most erudite art critic still responds with emotion. Paintings that have a strong impact on that critic will emotionally affect him, too.

We often see less beauty in things we encounter every day because these objects have simply lost their emotional impact. Those who see beauty in simple things usually have a stronger emotional response; they can still feel something about the pen they write with every day, or the dew on the grass on their lawn. Those for whom beauty is fleeting are often more affected by beauty when they see it; the emotion builds over time and is then released more strongly when it finally breaks free.

We're all a bit different. We see beauty through our own eyes, and we appreciate it in our own way, but we all love beauty when we find it. Beauty? It's what we see. It's what we love. It's what we love to see.

report to the home planet

I have spent the last several days with a task I have procrastinated away for thirty years now. I've been putting off fulfilling my mission but given the recent spate of free time, I felt it was finally the proper moment to assemble a brief report explaining to the folks back home on neptune, all of what I have learned of your people. I submit it humbly, here, on my space, out of consideration that you may want to know what is being said about you as a species, to those who are so distant.

My fellow Neptunians The following list encompasses the majority but not the totality of what I have learned of humankind, in the previous thirty years of observation and experimentation. I hope it will prove useful in your understanding of this place, and of the strange transmissions you have previously received from this place, which were the motivation for my original visit. I know that it has been quite some time since I reported to you; but as they say here, some things came up. I would like to present this information in list form, to ease my own thought process.

1.Human beings have some logical faculties.

2.They are usually set aside immediately whenever emotion is involved.

3.Their offspring individually, mean more to them than the destruction of their entire race.

4. Their convenience means more to them than their offspring's future standard of living.

5.This contradiction is resolved by arguing, screaming, carrying signs around, nursing infants in public, and sorting garbage into different containers within the home.

6. Human beings have an innate sense of inadequacy and guilt, which can easily be invoked to alter their behavior.

7. They enjoy this, but resent their own enjoyment of it, and rebel in curious ways. here I must digress to tell a story I heard which is native to this planet.

An archaeologist (refer to glossary at end) was seeking an ancient burial ground on the property of a tribal reservation. Several natives were watching him. He spied a mound, and grew excited. "Dig here!" he shouted to the natives. They raised their eyebrows at each other, shrugged, and fell to assisting him. As the hole grew they stopped helping, one by one, and stepped away. The archaeologist dug his pick into the dirt once again and fell into a slimy pit filled with human excrement. "Help me out!" he screamed. The natives helped him out of the hole. "What the hell was that???" he cried. "Oh, that's our new septic tank." The oldest of the men replied. "Why didn't you tell me that!" he asked, shaking his feces-coated arms wildly. "You never asked." Replied the sage.

8. Since the planet has slavery in various forms throughout its past and presetn, rebelling through obedience has become prevalent.

9.The vast majority of humans have never killed anything more than an insect. yet they consider themselves very dangerous, and are frightened of each other.

10.the male of the species, while it can be provoked to violence, is usually too concerned with sexual matters to be aggressive for any other reason.

11.The female of the species can be provoked, but will usually react with discomfort and shock to violence.

12. There are exceptions, of course, but the exceptions must have years of solid training before they can kill without fear. Even then, their shame is obvious to a keen observer.

13. In the western hemisphere, and part of the east, most people are concerned more with the objects they have accumulated than with anything else.

14. They become as emotionally attached to objects as they do to living things, if not more.

15. Many television shows, called "sitcoms", mock this tendency, especially in the male of the species, who are referred to as owning "toys".

16. The female of the species have the same compulsion, usually dedicated to objects which can be worn upon, or secreted in, the person.

17. Human beings communicate through an advanced series of gestures and sounds. Pure language is known to them, but few bother to use written language or telepathy. Most use a sort os primal body language, combined with repetitive phrasing.

18.Human beings are innately lazy, and this is dangerous because of its highly infectious nature as a meme. Convenience and speed are more valued by them than accuracy.

19 Though they have craftsmen and artisans, these usually produce useless tchotchkes and bits of unattractive artwork.

20. Their artists, visionaries, and poets are usually starved and emotionally attacked until dead. Then, they are valued highly.

21. They use a system in many areas, politically, economically, and socially, that pits the many against the few. Those who are most in need of protection or aid are "voted out" and those whose ideas could reverse bad group decisions are not permitted the power to do so.

22. Human beings do not like those who are more intelligent than them.

23. Human beings do not like those who are more attractive than them.

24 Human beings, in short, do not like anything, or anyone, who is better than them, in any capacity, whatsoever, and will often sabotage such, in order not to feel powerless and inadequate. (see #6, above)

25. Most will choose something useless and pretty that is cheap, to something functional and beautiful that is well-made.

26. They prefer to discard objects and acquire new ones, to maintaining or building those that will last.

27. The quickest way to a human's heart is through their greed for reassurance.

This concludes the first section of my report. In the next section, I've simply collected some tidbits from the popular culture of the western world, specifically the northern half of the north american continent.

People like to watch other people cry. Crying, especially attractive women crying, is one of the most common sights on their television. People enjoy hearing bad news about their bodies. They also enjoy hearing about simple and convenient ways to remedy these problems. Pills and medications, along with simple household tips, and cooking programs that refer to weight loss, are incredibly popular here.

People seem to be addicted to the minutest details of the interpersonal relationships of fictional characters. Not only do they argue, scream, cry, and nurse in public themselves, they will spend endless hours watching complete strangers pretend to do the same. People like unhealthy foods, and try to slowly kill themselves in a variety of ways.

Anything that is promoted with "regular joe" phrasing has immediate success.

People will more willingly vote for or purchase goods or services from an idiot than for or from an intelligent and rational person. People will resist any suggestion intended to modify their behavior, unless the reward is so great that it is impossible to resist. For some, this reward need not be large.

People will more willingly debase and degrade themselves for a prize, than they will uplift and protect their integrity, for the same prize. People like to watch other people fight and have sex, in that order.

People enjoy seeing those who disagree with them being harmed.

One facet of human life that still baffles me is the religious component. Although presented rationally on rare occasion (as a private matter of personal belief and deep feeling) usually it is with anger, hatred, and disgust at the world around them. It seems that most religious people of all faiths dislike sex, especially their particularly tabooed form, dislike festivities, dislike eroticism, dislike open speech and discussion, dislike intelligence, and are fervently opposed to change in any and all forms. This causes some public health issues, as well as many wars and other atrocities. I will attempt another report on this subject soon, after I have delved deeper.

labor day.

It's labor day.

I know you all are pretty much convinced that unions and the labor movement are some kind of terrible plague that has befallen the poor, beleagured captains of industry. That Unions somehow rape and kill thousands of workers, and that they may be single-handedly responsible for the high incidence of herpes in our younger people today. But in fact, unions have done many things for us, things even a non-employee un-wage-slave-type like me can appreciate.

They stopped employers from forcing workers to work in unsafe and possibly fatal conditions. Do you know anyone your own age who has black lung, reproductive radiation disorders, or heavy metal poisoning? I don't.

They forced employers to stop hiring children.

You know all those brats sitting at the bus stop playing their xbox, or stealing candy from the mini-mart, or hopping trains to freedom? They don't work 14 hour days, do they?

Well, maybe not everything the unions have done is a good thing.

Speaking of 14 hour days, when was the last time any hourly-wage worker you know pulled five of those in a row without overtime? I'm not talking about salary guys here. When's the last time a day's worth of work bought you a single meal? Actually, when's the last time you got paid less than minimum wage (not that minimum wage is one you could survive on...but you know what I'm saying)

Labor day, christmas, hannukah. MLK day. You know, holidays. There's a reason you aren't working until 4 am those days (if your employer is a big one.) Aren't you fucking lucky?

Well, no. No, you're not lucky. Hundreds of people fought their hardest with their bare fists, got their heads cracked open, died, so you could fucking complain that "minimum wage makes it hard on small businesses" or that "health benefits should be a matter of choice" or that "it's socialism"…well, so fucking what. Put your brats to work in the coal mine, if you love your masters so much. Give up your health. Give up your comfortable middle-class existence…because if the people that own you had their way, you'd live at the bare minimum to fund their caviar parties.

If you think the ethics of profit have changed since the 30s you are fooling yourself. There are people on this earth who do not care, who are only concerned with what they can put in their pocket. They're held back by a thin, unsecured fence, a fence the labor movement put up years ago…to protect you from their pillage. And if you don't appreciate that, maybe you deserve to live in the cardboard box and work the seventy-hour workweek at slave wages.

dr seuss, childfreedom.

I am childfree, and do not feel comfortable around, nor interested in, kids.

They disturb my mind in many ways. I do not have interest in them.

I do however remain childlike as myself; my life is lived even now as a Ville Villekulla, a bright and giddy place full of friends and art and craft and fun, and freedom. I like the way I dreamed I would live when I was a child. I have built the life of my youthful daydreams into reality around me like a coiled shell.

It satisfies me.

Dr. Seuss had little interest in children. He found them disturbing to his peace of mind, he stated that he was opposed to the population boom, and he rarely made time for children in his life. He and his wife had no children, didn't want them. He lived in his imaginary world IN REAL LIFE, and the cares and concerns and woes that a child requires would not allow those things to stand. So he stayed away from children, for the most part.

"Adults are just obsolete children and the hell with them both.""~Dr. Seuss

He did not enjoy the noise and commotion of children, and thought that perhaps if they were encouraged to use their minds and their imaginations instead of screeching and leaping around, they would become more capable and interesting adults one day.

"This book is to be read in bed."

? Dr. Seuss

Theodore Giessel was a very active man with unlimited skills in doggerel and inking strange creatures to fit. He was childfree- he had no children and wanted none.

Unless someone like you cares a whole awful lot, nothing is going to get better. It's not.

He once said "You have the kids, and I will entertain them."

While he was uninterested in children in person, he tapped in to their inner, imaginary abilities with his books and art. His own unfettered imagination, his freedom artistically and in his daily life, allowed him to live easily and create his work steadily. He feared fascism, was concerned deeply with overpopulation, and was in favor of legalizing abortion. He was a liberal, and was not averse to the socialist movement.

"I know, up on top you are seeing great sights, but down here at the bottom we, too, should have rights."

? Dr. Seuss, Yertle the Turtle and Gertrude McFuzz

I myself don't want children and have little or no interest in them. However it has been brought to my attention repeatedly that some of the art I make is loved, and well-loved by children whose parents have purchased it from me. The animals I draw hang in nurseries and in playrooms. The kids love the colors and the animals, and make up stories about them.

When I was very young, I had a set of animal cards. I loved these more than anything. Imagining all the animals in the wild, how I would meet them or get to pet or talk with them. Their behavior, learning about their way of living. It fascinated me.

I think that feeling and wonder I have for the creatures shows through enough, that imaginative children can feel it, and find it, and build their own inner worlds from it. I hope they can. Finding your imagination is a wonderful thing, and while I am against having more children at this time for anyone (7 billions! It's mind-boggling!) the children that are here, should be able to let their minds grow, and teach their brains to wander and imagine.

In short, neither I nor Dr. Seuss hate children. We simply prefer not to have them in our immediate personal lives. And while I do not want children of my own, I find that I can even so contribute to their growth and their futures by showing them that an imagination is the best thing in the world to carry with you.

MOTIVATIONS

to-do list

take your old blankets and towels and any pet toys or things to the local no-kill shelter. If you have time, volunteer to walk the dogs, or play with the cats.

take all your canned food that you didn't eat or use down to food for lane county or the food bank... especially if it's good stuff.

take all your books that you've already read, to the local literacy center. in eugene there's one downtown that teaches people to read.

take your old clothes, wash em, and give them to goodwill.

volunteer to go to a nursing home and visit people who don't have relatives that visit. You can offer to record memoirs (often single people without kids have led very interesting lives) let someone who looks more tired than you have your seat. Everyone can do something. Seriously.

I don't have a lot of time but I do what I can, and politics have nothing to do with it.

the dream.

I've been thinking a lot lately about my own past. Shady, strange, and not in any way direct...I've gotten here by a crazily side-winding route which would make no sense to anyone who had not walked it. I usually don't understand it myself.

I'm here to rant. But what I really want to talk about is living the dream.

You remember the dream. It's what you wished you'd be doing when you grew up. What you pictured your most awesome life looking like. What you wanted before you became too mature to daydream. Whatever happened to that? If you're not doing that right now, why the hell not?

Did you forget? Did you let other people tell you how to live? Have you given up your self, your soul, for the sake of...someone or something else? ARE YOU LIVING YOUR OWN LIFE, or someone else's?

I have no sympathy for you, if your life isn't your own. I never asked you to give it away, and if you know me you've probably heard a rant from me before about how I think you should do exactly whatever the hell YOU want. I'm a big believer in self-determination. If you haven't used your life for your own purposes, that was your choice, nobody else's. See, the scary thing, really, is that it WAS your choice to give away your time, to do things you didn't want. To not live for yourself. You made that choice.

The beautiful thing about living is that it's a constant shift. You get to change your mind, at any time, about just about anything you do. If you haven't been living your own damn life, now's the time to start.

It's hard to say no. It's hard to tell people you don't want to engage. Or that you're busy. Sometimes people take this the wrong way- the wrong people take it the wrong way every time. But you might be surprised at how well many of your friends will understand. I've always found the people that are the busiest, the most in love with whatever it is they're doing at the moment, these people are my favorite people. The people that REALLY CARE about what they DO. Whether that's reading, building, creating, adding up, riding, climbing, talking…they have a passion and they are actively chasing it.

It doesn't have to be earth-shattering.

It doesn't matter what you want to do. Just find something that you like, and give it as much of yourself as you can. You should be enjoying your life, while you have it.

art is life.

The world is a very grey and dismal place at times. There are deaths, horrors. We are all alone in these little bodies, floating around, disconnected most of the time- from each other and from the ground we stand on. Most people DO live quietly, desperately, working and thinking and amassing a thousand new worries each day.

Most people walk around afraid, nervous. Or angry. Or just focused on the task at hand, which for more people all the time involves merely surviving the vicissitudes of economy and thrift, of bad jobs or no work. Of struggle. Life is mostly struggle and concern for most people on earth, and for the rest it can be even worse.

It's our job, as artists, to show people that there is more. I am not a religious person, nor even a spiritual one. I do not believe that there is a sky-man or any kind of conscious entity watching over us carefully, or interested in our problems. I do not believe. BUT- I do believe that the world itself is a being of grace, and by truly seeing it, and being within it, we can lighten our weight. This entails details.

When one is in a chain gang, there will be a beautiful weed sprouting in the ditch. When one has lost hope and is starving, there will be the smell of dry morning air, and the sunrise. When the worries about the future become too much, there is still the present.

I know this doesn't make up for any of it. I also know that there are times for all of us when we realize our solitude, when we are alone and in pain, in the dark. Cold and possibly hopeless. In those times it is art's job to expose the alternatives, to bring the world into us and that way bring us out of ourselves.

Art doesn't have to be "good" or skilled or perfect or even beautiful to do this. It will be a different view for each artist and a different piece that speaks to each viewer. Sometimes the crude and the ugly do this much more effectively than the pretty and the sweet- actually for me, when I am alone and in pain in the dark, it is the reminder that others have been there as well that helps. And art that speaks this way is often NOT beautiful to look at.

I need to sell art to live- to pay rent. To eat. If I could give it away and not be homeless I would. But the necessities of the world insist that my work must be valued at a number. I know that for some the value of their work is low and their hours are long and hard; that they must do work which is difficult, upsetting, dangerous. I am lucky to be an artist, I am privileged in ways not many are. I love my work. That alone is a stroke of fortune.

People who hate their work but must do it deserve my best efforts, because I know that at times my work, seeing my work and interacting with it, is their release and their reminder. Artists have an obligation to try their damnedest to do that, and to do it as best they can every time.

wealth

From the moment when the machine first made its appearance it was clear to all thinking people that the need for human drudgery, and therefore to a great extent for human inequality, had disappeared. If the machine were used deliberately for that end, hunger, overwork, dirt, illiteracy and disease could be eliminated within a few generations. ...

But it was also clear that an all-round increase in wealth threatened the destruction - indeed, in some sense was the destruction - of a hierarchical society. ... the most obvious and perhaps the most important form of inequality would already have disappeared.

If it once became general, wealth would confer no distinction. ... But in practice such a society could not long remain stable. For if leisure and security were enjoyed by all alike, the great mass of human beings who are normally stupefied by poverty would become literate and would learn to think for themselves; and when once they had done this, they would sooner or later realize that the privileged minority had no function, and they would sweep it away.

holidays in general.

I love holidays.

I once dated a man that hated holidays. I should have known this was a bad sign. I like holidays. I remember arguing hard in favor of having even a wreath in the house in winter. "But you're not religious, even!" he'd say. "You hate that shit! Besides, it's kind of a consumer-whore thing, this holiday..."

He thought Valentine's day was created solely to make him look stupid. That Xmas was made specifically as an insult to his ability to choose gifts for people. (Of course, he was poor at gift-giving. He didn't like being made to think about other people and what they might want.) He thought New Year's was a joke, and July 4th was just a way for rednecks to blow their hands off. I went two years without a new year's kiss, without a date on v-day, without a prank on april 1st-to some people that seems like no big deal, but for a rabid sentimentalist romantic holiday person like me it's depressing. Why did I stick around? He used my brain against me, that's why.

I can see the reason he'd think all these things. I'm not foolish. I know, I know. Being a material, greedy, consumer is bad. Thinking that love can be shown by buying things doesn't really appeal to me, either. My dog gets scared when fireworks go off. I don't like obnoxious drunks. All of his arguments were completely valid, in a way, rational. I started to feel foolish for caring about these dumb things, these mass-media shenanigans, these marketing strategies. Had I been a fool? Had I been taken in by all the things I hated? Was I – as he called it- a sheeple? All of my inner joy was shriveling under the harsh glare of analysis. I couldn't justify myself in my fun. I had no excuse, and irony pointed its long, cruel finger at me and laughed.

Irony, I hate her. She's such a bitch and she never lets her hair down.

I am no longer in the grips of all that, thankfully. That was years ago, in the before-times. I don't respect the distanced pose that those thoughts encouraged. I respect letting loose a little more now(within reason-I still think too much. Don't get scared)

So, we come full circle to the holidays.

I don't give xmas presents. I don't want any, really. Every year I make a list and put it out there. Usually more than half of it is non-material things that nobody could buy for me, like love, lust, steady hands. Sometimes I put stuff on the list too, but I don't expect it…or really want that stuff, for that matter. I have too much stuff as it is. But I like the idea of giving. Spending time with people you like, telling people good things, being warm.

I like xmas lights, I like festivities. xmas is a nice day. Solstice is even better. I wrap my head around the fact that now, solstice, the days will be long again! We're heading back toward summer now, and swimming, and sunshine. This is worth celebrating. I also LOVE new year's. I like it when something new starts. I like laughing, I like loads of people cheering, I like a kiss.

I like candles in the window and dreidels. I like Mr. Magoo. Hell yeah! Rich people sharing! What a concept! I like Santa. I really do. Santa is awesome ... Also, I still, to this day, put out a plate for him. Of course now it's a grown-up plate. And of course now I just ask him in my note for good luck, and lots of love, and good ideas for art, so he doesn't have to tote anything heavy into my house.

You don't like xmas? Well, fine. I find jeebus a little offensive, too. But it's not about jeebus or about buying crap. Try not buying a damn thing for anyone. Just eat food and talk kindly to the people you know. Just hug someone (even if like me you HATE hugs) and spend a little time thinking about other people and what they might want. Celebrate Hanukkah, Kwanzaa, solstice. I do solstice. But I say "merry xmas, happy holidays, etc"...why get pissed? try to think about other people ! and what they might want! they want you to smile at them and say happy holidays. merry xmas. joyful kwanzaa. awesome solstice. something!

That's how you do the winter holidays. You don't have to justify being happy. You're allowed, for fuck sake. It's all right to enjoy something whole-heartedly, even if other people think it's stupid. Who cares? You're happy, right? That's what matters. You're not ever gonna regret being happy just for yourself. You will never look back and say "I wish I hadn't let myself be happy that day."

motivated.

I like what I do.

It took a long time to get better at it (and I'm still only pretty good, and during most of my life I have come across as a cynical, pessimistic person. I've usually played down whatever I was doing that was good or that I thought was awesome, just so as not to jinx things. I've jinxed stuff before and I don't like it.

But through all of it I think I've always held deep inside a fundamental sense that things will eventually, somehow just be OK and that whatever I was doing at the time, as long as I enjoyed it, it made me happy, then all the rest would work itself out.

You have to decide what you like. That's the hard part. I happen to like orange, so I painted my house orange inside. I mean, I rent, but fuck it, right? As long as it's left how I got it... it can be orange as long as I live here. So bright orange, bright baboon-ass red, straight shock pink. All next to each other. I also like having tons of fun things laying around to pick up and make art or play with. So it's kind of a haphazard mess of weird instruments, odd bits of plastic, paints. I live in Ville Villekula.

And why not? Who else spends as much time in my space as I do? Who else is paying for it? Nobody, that's who. It's home. It has to make me happy.

Work is the same way. You have to know what you like. Do a lot of that thing, like tons, everyday. Even if you're tired the fuck out from getting up at 5 AM to sell newspapers to yuppies (true story from my own past) you still gotta drink another cup of coffee and go ahead and write, draw, paint, tattoo, ride a bike, cliff dive, cook. Whatever it is you like doing. Because that's why you're alive, that thing, whatever it is. If you get hurt and you can't do it any more then you explain to other people the things you learned that made it something you liked. If you can still use your eyes and hands and legs you have no excuse, you just gotta do what you like and keep doing it. Tons of it.

Work might be how you pay rent and not something you love but if you do what you like hard enough and often enough and get really good at it, then it doesn't matter if you earn your living that way or not, really. Because it becomes the center of your life either way. I mean it's great if you can end up quitting your day job and doing something rad for a living but honestly as long as you get to do tons of what you like that's what matters.

And if you don't know what you like you gotta just start trying crap out. Try everything even if it sounds stupid as hell. Go along with someone who knows how and ask stuff and try things. If you try about a hundred things you'll probably find one thing you like, or at least one thing you're ok at, and maybe even something that you like AND are ok at.

Life gets better after a while, then it sucks, then it's awesome, then it's torture, then it rocks, then it's awful, then it's bearable, then it's ok, then it's pretty good and then the next thing you know you're dead anyway and everybody else just keeps on going. You may as well do what you like with your life. Nobody else owns it, after all. Nobody else spends as much time in it, or works hard to pay for it, but you.

ambition.

I want to get more motivated. I want to be less lazy. I want to do better, work harder, grab the day each day and fucking DO SHIT RIGHT...I don't wanna look back later on and wish I was more motivated and more driven and less lazy and afraid...I wanna conquer the world

I see my friends getting better all the time, my colleagues outpacing me, growing, doing things I wish I could do...working, doing amazing stuff

people growing all the time. the seattle convention made me wish I was way better than I am. I don't know where to start except to sink my fingers in to the knuckles and grab hold, and ride

I'm gonna work way harder way more often, I gotta catch up to my people and pass them, I want to be as inspiring to them as they are to me

someone told me over the weekend that they were surprised that with my attitude and interests that my book had a lot of flowers and bright lightness in it and foofoo things. they are right. I don't get to do the kind of images I really like, things I like, as often as I want to

skulls, blood, gore, zombies, satans, devil, naked chicks...the scary stuff...I need to put myself into my work more, my secret self, and not be afraid that I'll go broke

I know there has to be people like me, who like that kind of stuff, out there,...I know I can do it

I just gotta work really hard, hope that everyone helps me out when I need it, gives me directions to the place I want to be.

today.

Today is the only day we have, we don't have tomorrow, the next day. Only today.

Will we regret, later on, not having done everything we could, as hard, as strong, as much as we could? YES!!! We will regret it! LIVE NOW, now is the time. We have today! Today is amazing! Action is in the air, sparks are everywhere, and there's no reason not to do EVERYTHING!

Life is for living! Go outside! Run around! Paint, draw, sing, dance, scream, party, rage, laugh, leap!!! DO SOMETHING because you won't ever get today again! EVER! You have to use it up right now! You may as well laugh and jump and have fun, do cool things, throw your body around like it's made of rags and stitches! LIVE IT UP, living is so good for you. Doing the things you love is what your life is for!

If you have to work, work as fun and as hard and as well as possible, don't do things half-assed, you don't get to live twice! DO IT ALL THE WAY THE FIRST TIME! If you're in love LET GO AND GIVE IT ALL YOU'VE GOT! If you're mad beat someone up! If you're sad CRY LOUD!

Today means everything. It'll never be today again! It'll be gone! You'll have wasted it! You won't regret doing everything as hard and as much as possible, you won't, I promise! Years from now you won't sit around thinking "I wish I'd been more lazy, and less motivated!" I PROMISE!!!

You don't need more SPARE time, you need more ACTION! We all need to use it up! All of it! Don't waste a drop! I mean it, I'm serious as hell right now, throw yourself in, because you're stuck here anyway!

It's the best day! TODAY!

money laundering.

Apparently, you can launder money by buying art. I have never had dirty money, so I wasn't aware of this. (All three of my dollars have been squeaky-clean.) I'm just putting it out there- if anyone has a few millions laying around in torn cardboard boxes behind their drywall, mucky as hell, I'm willing to let you buy my work, then use it to explain where all that cash came from.

I mean, someone's got to help the needy cash hoarders, right?

Knuckle sandwich

COMPLAINTS

bad days.

Now, I am going to discuss something most artists hate to admit. Bad Days.

We all have them. Once in a while everyone wakes up on the wrong side of the bed, breaks a nail, has bad hair, steps in dog shit, car won't start, etc, etc. Most people go to work, hang tight, and eventually the bad mood fades. Not so for tattoo artists.

Our work's quality depends upon our ability to be friendly, be focused, and be creative. If your juices aren't flowing it doesn't really matter how much we might usually like you or your tattoo art…it just sucks to have to smile when you're having a bad day.

I think most artists work throughout the bad days-they just stuff it in, try to forget it, bottle it up…I see a lot of work that isn't as good as the artist's usual work, and wonder…We all have bad days. For a tattoo artist that can mean that someone is wearing your second-best effort for the rest of their life.

My usual solution is to try to call in sick. Or something to the effect-I take extra time away from work, I reschedule people, I stay away from tattooing until the mood passes, and then I come into the shop with a fresh perspective. This is usually in my client's best interest. More often than not I feel bad, or guilty about rescheduling people. This makes me try harder with the artwork. Makes me try harder to hurt them less. Makes me try to make up for them waiting so long. Also I'm no longer in a bad mood. I'm happy to be there, my creativity is more available to me. This makes my work better in so many ways-I'm willing to take a little longer to get it just right-to try something new that will improve the finished product. Also my drawings just seem to turn out better with less effort when I am in a good mood about being at work.

Some people get very angry about this shuffling. I mean, I understand. The day you're supposed to get tattooed is a big deal! You took off work, you skipped a class, you canceled plans…and there you are, happy, excited, nervous, ready to pay big money that took forever to save up…and the artist's not ready? Or asks if it's ok to change the day or time? I have been there too, on that side of it. I am a tattoo artist, but I am also a tattoo client. I have tons of work. I have been bumped, rescheduled, canceled on, all of it. And it sometimes upset me.

I guess I'm just talking, wasting time and space here by saying it, but try (like I try) to keep in mind that you definitely want your artist bright-eyed and eager to tattoo you. If that means waiting a few more days, it usually is better to go ahead and wait. If it means that you will get better quality work, then it is definitely worth the wait. The experience of the process of getting a tattoo only lasts a little while, but you'll be looking at the art forever. . .

Also remember that your artists is, indeed, human. We get tired, burned out, have surgery, our girlfriends get sick, our dogs die, and our cars break down too. Just like your life we have things outside of work that we care about. Try to be patient with us, because most of us are less grounded than most people. We're artists, too, and that makes us weird. So please be patient with us…we're trying! We do appreciate it a lot when people are willing to be patient, and when you are understanding…just like you would.

MAGICAL BULLSHIT.

Usually I have no interest in magic (beyond watching old penn and teller shit from before they became all seriously-minded) (and beyond the hilarity of a magician named GOB) but my partner is on a magic kick right now, and so he had this thing written by angel, and in it...a whole chapter about the worst pain of his life and how he endured it.

A six-point, medium-gauge, suicide suspension. six-point=six hooks, which means the weight is distributed more, which means each hook is less painful. It looks like six-gauge hooks in the picture- which are not that big, but big enough to keep any skin from tearing. Basically, the easiest, most beginner way to suspend. Something any soccer mom could likely do (if she felt like it)

None of the stuff involving standard piercing, tattooing, or suspensions like the one angel underwent, are really painful at all compared to things most people experience all the time-by choice- such as sustained exercise like marathons, childbirth, walking all day in heels, giving blood, etc etc...if you have ever broken a bone you have been through far worse than any of this stuff, by a LONG shot. If you've ever had a cut that needed stitches you've been through worse. seriously.

I haven't suspended a million times or anything- but I spend a lot of time watching people suspend. At gatherings, at shops, at conventions, at performances. I've seen a lot of different reactions and a lot of different kinds of people try it.

Now, because I have watched so many people suspend, and because I have seen the full range of reactions to it, I can honestly claim that suspending in the manner he did is FAR from horrifying. I mean, shit, yeah it hurts some. But not anything like what he writes about. It sounds pretty much like self-aggrandizing bullshit to me. And as if he would like to seem way more out-there than suspensions actually ARE.

Maybe he is trying to appeal to the demographic which thinks tattoos are death-defying and require a sedative? that piercing is horrific? That stretching your ears is called "gauging" and involves some kind of medieval torture?

People, normal everyday people, do much more intense suspensions than the one he did, all while smiling and joking around and smoking a cigarette, yelling "I'm flyingggg!!!" and spinning or swinging around like the ropes are a personal swing set. Normal, nonfreaky, unmagical people. I've seen judges, doctors, soccer moms, chefs, librarians, strippers, respected journalists, office workers, and tons of normal people climb a rope for fun.

I'm not sure, but I can say this much. It's crap. He is basically more of a total pussy than some little librarian girls and big fat chef dudes I know, who live normal boring lives and happen to have done several suspensions without even dropping a tear.

Has the man never been injured? If that is the worst pain he has ever experienced- I am very envious of his sheltered life.

It's just strange to me that he'd even bother.

at any rate, I've been told the rest of the book is pretty much him kissing his own ass anyway. so I guess it works for him...right?

the NRA.

I don't really think I need to re-state my position on gun control laws, since it's obvious that I am a gun owner, and that I think owning weapon is a right, not a privilege.

However, I want to re-state them anyway.

I think everyone who has not committed a violent crime should be permitted to own whatever weapons they choose, without having to register them or alert the government. I see the need for background checks; it only takes ten minutes to run a name and see any violent convictions on someone's record. I see no need for waiting periods, for anything else.

I am very, very lefty. I'm basically a retired anarchist; I would still love to live in a gift economy, but I do not think this can happen during my lifetime, so I've modified my actions based on what I think is possible to accomplish.

I believe in spending public funds on welfare, schools, higher education, and healthcare for all citizens. I believe that religion has no place in ANY publicly-funded system or in ANY politics. I think that people who want abortion to be illegal are idiots. I think that patriarchy is bad, that our culture is set up in many wrong ways. I believe in class warfare, unions as a concept, the rights of workers, and of the underclass to act out. I dislike the way we use our military to screw up other areas of the world, and I think our policies are a direct result of corruption and patriarchy. In other words, I'm not right-wing, I am NOT republican, and I am NOT in favor of god, the bible, and apple pie. I'm basically a commie pinko.

So- while I agree with some things the gun lobbyists stand for- such as my right, and everyone else's right to bear arms- I can't donate any money to them, can't support them in any way, because when I go to an NRA site and see people rooting for assholes who would put me in prison for my reproductive choices, or touting some bullshit flag-waving nonsense about how we should bomb "camel jockeys", or condescension to female members or participants-

Well, that just sucks, and all of that is what I am against, and passing laws to restrict what I can do with my body is just as repressive as passing laws to restrict what weapons and means of defense I can own, and you guys, THAT is some BULL SHIT. Women want to bear arms too. As do socialists, abortion providers and people who have had abortions, pro-choice folks, people who aren't in favor of recent wars, people who dislike racism and sexism- we carry too. So putting us down on the regular is just foolish.

body shame.

Lately, I've been seeing a lot of stuff addressing the lack of larger or fat women in advertising, as symbols of beauty. It's good in a way to see more of this, because the focus on one body type in media can be really disturbing. The implications that anyone bigger than the models is sick, lazy, or unhealthy; that fat women are all ugly, these aren't right and need changing. I really think it's good to raise awareness about body image, and to show women of all different sizes as beautiful and feminine.

That said, I also find it disturbing that many of these essays portray thin women as "anorexic" "unreal" and "nonexistent". Look, I do know that the use of photoshop and the like has made images of impossible women pretty damn common. And yes, a lot of celebrities have eating disorders. But this isn't always the case. By portraying thin women as unhealthy, sick, or unreal, you are continuing body shame. You are doing the exact same thing to other women that media has done to you, and it's just as rotten .You're continuing the cycle of abuse. Yes, you. You were hurt, so now, you'll hurt others. For shame?

Thin women exist. Not all of them are anorexic. Many of them are scrawny, even. People vary. Some of us have high metabolisms, some have lower metabolism. Every size is beautiful; health is distributed equally across the scale. There are fat women who ARE lazy. There are thin women who DO puke after meals. But there are fat women who are healthy as hell and eat good food and are active, and thin women who eat well and have balanced lives.

You don't have to insult thin women to make fat women feel better. When you're talking about how offended you were by a sign at a gym (mermaid or whale?) you don't have to insinuate that whales are awesome and healthy and mermaids don't even exist, are asexual, and have body issues. I'm right here! I can hear you! I'm reading this thing you wrote because I AGREE with you, for fuck sake! Why are you telling me I'm unattractive? I think that sign was stupid too! But now- now I think you just don't get it. and I won't even get into how rude, how... UNFEMINIST, telling women that not getting pregnant makes them less important, is. Because that's an entire new can of worms. As if getting pregnant was part of beauty? It can be, for some. For others, it isn't. Why make either choice shameful? What the hell is wrong with you?

The same people who made that sign make signs saying I need to bulk up muscle. They try to sell supplements to me. They insinuate that being thin is unhealthy; they're trying to make money off of my shame AND yours. Why are you helping them? What's wrong with the shape I am? You and I can be different. Neither one of us has to feel like shit about it.

Stop telling women that the shape of their body is wrong somehow. Stop insulting other women. This makes you part of the problem.

Seriously. I agree with you. Quit alienating me because I am not fat. Calling me a skinny bitch, unreal, or anorexic is not helping matters. The same way I don't walk up to strangers in public and ask "How did you get so fat?" refrain from doing this kind of thing to me, in reverse.

I think fighting eating disorders is a noble goal. Women with eating disorders who are my size, however, STILL think they are fat. Eating disorders are not caused by size, but by mental illness, exacerbated by body shame. The same kind of body shame you are helping to spread.

Next time to sit down to write about how fat women need more respect, admiration, and acceptance, keep in mind that body shame is the root of it all. DON'T BE PART OF THE PROBLEM. Fight against body shame, not against other women who are shaped differently than you.

kafka.

When I die, please pile all of my creative work high on the pyre.
Burn it all down.
Please don't go through it all, re-edit and assemble it for sale,
and then make a million dollars from my sad,
overworked corpse.
Kafka was firmly of the opinion that if they don't want it now, while
it can do me some good to sell it, they can't have it later, the bastards.

He worked full-time, NOT as a writer, throughout his life. He would
come home tired from long workdays and stay up all night writing.

I'd have been pissed too. They always blame his lack of confidence in
his own work- but I think, deep down, it was his fury that he had had
to work so goddamn hard all the time while lesser authors had the
leisure and funds to write, and to enjoy their lives.

Every time you think "I wish he had written more" ask yourself-
when is the last time you PAID A CREATIVE PERSON for something, and
spread the word, so they'd have time to write or paint more? People
didn't pay HIM either, so there's your answer. He never had time,
because he had to pay the rent. That's how most creative people tend to
live- I am lucky because my day job is art too, but even so, it's not free,
it's not MY WORK wholly. Even so.

the woman.

What are you afraid of?
I mean, in your everyday life. What do you actually fear?
I personally am not afraid that someone in a hockey mask will chop
me to pieces at summer camp. I'm not really worried about zombies,
monsters, or mutated townsfolk in New Mexico wastelands. I don't
shudder to think that cave creatures will eat me, and I don't believe in

ghosts- not ghosty ghosts, anyway. I'm an atheist so demons don't frighten me.

Shit, what IS there to fear?

The things that scare me are things that are possible.

I used to get a scared thrill from serial killer sort of movies. Pioughkeepsie Tapes is a great example of this, and I liked it because I watch and read a lot of true-crime nonfiction. The cop's eye view, though- it makes another layer there, a bit of distance. No matter how the suspense that "the killer could be watching this with you in the theater" is attempted, those crimes are in the past, and therefore not something possible, something frightening.

Movies like "Henry" or "I Spit on Your Grave" are along these lines. The plot is possible, (though unlikely) and the themes of vulnerability are frightening. There's only so many times I can be frightened by the same slasher plot, so many times that the thought of a serial killer, the slim chance of that, can make me horrified. And if a film is a remake- for me, it barely counts. I have a hard time immersing myself in the film if I have seen it before. I spend my time looking for plot changes, comparing the new cast to the old, rather than suspending my disbelief.

So what actually scares me? When I see a movie with a character that is narcissistic, abusive- someone who is manipulative enough to pass as normal to others- I start to get a little scared. Domestic abuse scares the shit out of me. Rape and child abuse, neglect and sexual assault. Movies like A Serbian Film scare the crap out of me- those things happen, that stuff exists, and worse. And there are people all around who seem normal who pay per view...

So, given all this, The Woman is a great horror movie- and not just a great horror movie, but potentially a game-changer.

To have a female character not run, not once, not scream- during an entire movie. Regardless of how this is accomplished within the plot, it's a complete reversal of the usual characterization of women in horror films. The father's slick, brazen control over his family and his maltreatment of the women in it is believable, and familiar. The first slap is almost a release of the tension in the film. In an abusive relationship, every moment is spent in tension, waiting for the shoe to drop- and the movie does a great job of building that tension, and then releasing it.

Of course the ending is extreme. However there is one scene which stands out- as the Woman is killing the father, she pumps her arm inside his wound, staring into his eyes. It's definitely a sexual moment, a reversal, again, of the usual theme in horror. She's fisting his wound, violating him physically in a violent manner. Usually in horror only women are violated this way, and with this much eroticism to the violence.

The character of the son, with his nascent sociopathy and sadism, was absolutely chilling. Men who are as disturbed and abusive as the father in this film do NOT make good parents to daughters OR sons. It's questionable whether that character could have been redeemed at any point, whether it's in his genes or taught- but that he purposely explains his motives and actions to the son suggests it is both.

The mother's hopelessness in the situation and her seeming inability to do anything useful is very accurate. In an abusive relationship of long standing, the abused person becomes listless, unable to make decisions. The mother in this film has obviously been taught well that there is no hope for her; that there is no escape, and that her situation, bad as it is, is the best she will ever get.

This is horror. This is something that CAN happen. People like the father in this film exist, and they are not "crazy-looking", they are not wearing skin masks, out on the edge of society. They preach in the church and sell the real estate and run the bank. They are high-functioning and they exist. When they're caught, IF they are caught, nobody can believe it. Often the abused in the family are not believed. And through slow escalation, their abuses can eventually become extreme and unbelievable. I have to add this character to the list of accurately-depicted narcissists in film. He's apt, he's correct, and his casual ownership of others, his assumed control over them, is exactly how these people operate in real life.

The only real problems with this, for me, were the crappy, overclocked soundtrack (WAY TOO LOUD, wtf?) and the allowance of bits of humor in the violence and catharsis at the end. There is no reason to shy away and lighten the mood during a cathartic scene- just let the intensity stay high, please. Hitting the dog-sister in the head with a goofy "clang" doesn't add much to the scene, and dilutes the character of the woman into slapstick, instead of wordless menace.

I read a lot about crap like extreme neglect, and feral children, and I thought the main character was very well written on that level.

It's the first movie I've seen in a while, too, in which the bad guys did NOT look like cartoon versions of my friends, (*coughinsidiouscough*, *hic30daysofnightcup*) but like the kind of people I have known in real life to be completely rotten.

So- yes, it's a great horror movie. It scared the crap out of me, right up to the ending- which made me feel better. Just like any great horror movie, you get to ride away, while leatherface dances alone.

bechdick test.

The Bechdel test is simple. Your book, film, or other work passes if it contains two named female characters, who speak to each, about something other than a man (or men).

I actually think about this while reading or watching a movie. Some movies that have been hailed as feminist masterpieces (by morons *cough*) don't pass this test. And some movies I love but which are seen as just awful to women- DO pass.

The corollary I'd give, is that if your work doesn't pass the Bechdick test as well, you are off the hook. This second test is simple- if your film, book, or other work contains two men, with names, who speak to each other about something other than women, it has passed the test.

Some works contain only one character, two male characters, or a mixed pair. These works are officially off the hook, not liable to the test. Since they wouldn't pass the Bechdick test, you can't apply Bechdel to them either.

However, a book that passes one MUST pass the other as well, or it's simply not realistic. Even fantasy works should maintain enough realism in the characters to make me believe they are real, to flesh them out. If a work doesn't pass the Bechdel test, I find my suspension of disbelief waning, and my interest in the (male) characters almost lost-since some characters are not realistic, none can be.

Stephen King

dear Stephen King,

fuck sake. not every book has to be a continuation of another. the dark tower series was all right, yeah. but you're not tolkein and seriously, the people that get off on hearing "say thanked" and crap like that want you to keep writing one story again and again and that universe is stale now.

move on. you lived, dude. please just write more stories about stuff that scares you- it's getting ridiculous, like reading a different cujo for every dog breed, like kathy bates kidnapping twelve writers in a series, like you've turned into a cheap, cut-rate, cs lewis.

and you're not. the best things you've done are things that stand alone. a work of art that needs the artist standing next to it,explaining, isn't a good work at all.

I'm tired of your middle period. let's have the good stuff, please.

(1408 and maybe Duma Key, seem to lean in that direction.

although I could be wrong about that.)

thanks,

inconstant reader

-(yes, I know. Stephen King won't actually read this open letter.)

Let's talk about Desperation. Now...the book is not that great. It's extremely heavy handed on the God tip. I can understand the religiosity and madness of some of his later work (the tail end of the Dark Tower series and suchlike) because after all he was injured and likely suffering from PTSD at that time. This book, however, has no excuse.

King always appealed to me because his work rarely got too philosophical- beyond the portrayals of small town "normal people". In the work he did just before and after Desperation, he tended to start introducing himself, thinly veiled, as a character in his own work. The appearance of the godlike author in the Dark Tower series is the pinnacle of this nonsense.

Desperation has some redeeming elements as a book; the movie on the other hand...King wrote the teleplay of it. He did the adaptation and apparently had quite a bit of creative control. I won't draw any conclusions yet about whether or not this is the source of the trouble with some of his films; we'll wait until I get a chance to find a bit more information.

I know. He doesn't care really, what we all think of his work. He gets paid, right? I understand that he probably has little negative response at this point from anyone whose opinion matters to him. and he HAS written so much really good work that he may feel he doesn't have to worry so much anymore about the actual craft of scaring people. I mean, he's written an incredibly good book about horror writing himself. But...I just want more of the good stuff. You know? I get like this, critical, mostly because I used to love his work so much. And I don't read much pulp or paperbacks or genre fiction. I am a book person. A "real" book person. And I used to adore his books. Now, I find so many flaws in everything he writes. I know it's a bit demanding but I want more GOOD movies and books from this man- or I want to stop having my hopes dashed. And so I'm sitting here in a stenched out room, with the smell of my own sick sweat encasing me, watching Storm of the Century and wishing it was Cujo.

Storm of the Century. Yeah, let's talk about this one. Again, made for television. So again, we shouldn't get our hopes up. Like Desperation, it was adapted by King himself. And like Desperation, it is heavy on the godtalk. Also, the cgi is hit-or-miss, but I assume that even though King had a degree of creative control, this may not be entirely his fault.

The dialogue is unbearable. The acting is mediocre. But...the manner in which it is written is the downfall. Blunt, unsubtle speeches. A bad guy named "legion". I think that this, along with Desperation, belong more on the christian networks than in any nonreligious channel or network. Unscary to boot. As a non-religious person, the idea of demons or devils coming to get revenge on me for not praying just is NOT frightening. And no amount of heavy-handed bible talk is going to change that.

The Exorcist is a somewhat frightening religious movie. Desperation and Storm of the Century can't just repeat that format with different characters and be frightening. It's obsolete horror. It's old. It's been done, and better.

As usual he can write decent settings, but that's always been one of King's strong suits. Usually, that is. Let's talk about something else, instead.

Thinner, for example. Now, this book was all right. Not the top ten of King's; not great, but not awful. I am hyperthyroid and have a high metabolism and have always had trouble keeping weight on, so it at least had some element of body horror I found personally frightening. It again is very morally heavy handed and obvious- but at the same time a bit more obscure and undefined.

The movie isn't quite as terrible as the other two here- it's not really that well-acted in general, and the pacing is awful- but the screenplay and writing, the adaptation, is fairly well done. It was not adapted by

King. I've done as much research as internetting allows and it seems that King had little or less creative control over this one. My own personal opinion; The Shining (NOT THE REMAKE) is probably the best King-related movie made. And The Langoliers is most likely the worst.

Knuckle sandwich

TALES

the Brag.

I lived in a squat. This was the early 90s. I showered once a month at a woman's house I had befriended just for that purpose. It was worth it, she didn't ask for much from me and her apartment had plenty of hot water. She was one of those rich kids that hang off the punk scene like a fat tick, eating us a little at a time. But she let me shower and clean up there whenever I could bring myself to be in her company for a few hours.

The house I lived in had been a nice house at one time. Then some shitheel bought it and stopped maintaining it. It had been built when the neighborhood was nice, then it had become a hellish area riddled with crime, then been gentrified, then again become shot through with churches and liquor stores. The gas station on the corner had bulletproof glass and a little drawer through which you put your money. You had to gesture wildly at the fat korean guy in there to get him to put whatever you wanted back through the drawer. Usually he tried to put cigarettes in the drawer first no matter what you pointed at.

We'd moved in because the owner was so obviously absent. One of the guys I hung around with had heard that if a building had back taxes owed and you could squat it for two years you would own it. I personally thought this was bullshit but it was clear that nobody gave a shit about the building and it hadn't been taken care of in decades. Boarded up, coated in filth. We broke into a back window and unboarded the back door and moved all our shit into it. There were four or five of us at first but any time you put drugs into a free house more people show up, it's like a fungus, we turned into a crowd pretty quickly. There was a retarded guy, a guy who knew how to steal water, and a couple of girls that would sit on the floor and giggle back and forth. We had a really tall skinny guy there who did a bunch of repairs. One day he was in the kitchen cutting up two by fours we'd stolen from tis place down the street where they were building some kind of church. He was cutting them into sections so he could shore up a window better. At the time it was just covered with a piece of flimsy plywood and the wind kept coming in.

He knew how to use a saw so he was cutting. Long extension cord all across the room. Inevitably someone jerked the cord and he sliced off one of his fingers, his left index finger, right at the bottom. We searched all over for it for hours both before and after he left for the hospital. It had vanished completely and instantly. This was before the usual pack of smelly pit bulls had become resident at the house so there was only a vague possibility that it had been eaten.

We didn't find it until six months later. A few of us were peeling potatoes in the kitchen, getting ready to make one of those giant horrible stews that communal bums often make as dinner, and one of the bowls spilled, rolling these small potatoes all over the kitchen floor. I reached under the counter by the ground and grabbed something dry. When I pulled my hand out I was holding a twig, a twig with a flat end covered in a fingernail. It was such a clean cut at the bottom that I was surprised.

"I found your finger, man."

"HELLS yeah! Do you think they can still put it back on?"

He wore it around his neck on a shoestring for a long time. I think he lost it again later shooting dice at a show, and ended up betting it with someone, who won and took it away from him.

And then, there was the run of visiting corpses. We had a few dead guests, most of whom did not die at or in the house, but who were brought there, already stiff, to hang around with us. This became a point of disagreement for a while.

In our squat, we held shows once in a while. This was pretty common at the time, there was another couple of squats in town, one in north philly near us that had had a great show with tribe 8 and size queen, and another in west philly where nausea and born against played.

At that show I'd been taken in after being too drunk, I couldn't have gotten across town alive in my state. I'd leaned against a wall and vomited down into the sleeve of my own leather jacket, in an attempt to seem sober enough to go home. Luckily they stopped me. The next day I used their hose to blow the vomit out of my coat sleeve, drank one of their warm beers, and walked all the way back to the other side of the city.

There are some things I miss about those times in my life but the smell of vomit is not one of them. We had woken up around one or two in the afternoon and my walk took me until sundown, I was slow, tired, I had quit doing hard drugs the week before and had not regained my equilibrium yet. I wobbled my way through the suspicious yuppies in center city and up north to my house.

I'd just gotten home, in the late afternoon, re-rinsed my jacket and laid it out on the porch. I was sitting on the porch drinking a beer and smoking, watching the sun go down, when two of my squatmates walked up the street, with a third person suspended between them. Weekend at Bernie's style, dragged, between them.

A retarded guy with a crooked mohawk and an angry, nihilist-type political anarcho-punk named Dan who had an indescribable information-society-style haircut which combined dreadlocks, bald spots, and tufts. It was a ragged trio even to my jaded and crusted eyes. His feet were top down dragging on the pavement. His arms were awkward around their shoulders.

He looked pretty fucked up.

"Who the fuck is that?" I asked them. I didn't want another milk-in-the-tub incident.

"We met him last night, he was sick at the show, we've been walkin home with him all day." said Dan, smiling. My retarded friend piped up "We took him in the bus but we missed the stop so we were in west philly! WAY WEST PHILLY!"

He smiled, proud that they'd been able to bring the guy home safely anyway.

I walked up closer and tapped the guy's chest with my knuckles. "He's cold, guys. I think he's dead."

"He's NOT. No WAY." Dan was hung over and red eyed, already pissed off at me. "He's MY NEW FRIEND and he's COMING IN to have a BEER."

"You are not bringing a dead body into my fucking house. No fucking way."

We stood leaning in at each other. I was a lot smaller than him but then again, I wasn't holding up a dead body. The dead guy's head was lolled to the side a little and I could see that his eyes were open, empty, and unmoving.

"You can bring him in if he wakes up, even moves his eyes or blinks."

"FINE." Dan and my friend set the guy down on the steps. His body stayed kind of straight, and didn't bend to conform to the stairs.

Dan shook the guy, "Wake up man, you gotta wake up or we can't go inside!" This went on for a long time. Eventually I went inside and left them, the three of them. At one point my friend came inside to ask for a glass of milk, which I told him wouldn't help. At another point another squatmate came home, a girl named Joony that had moved in, and I could hear her high-pitched voice shouting, joining, trying to wake the guy up.

I went to bed and forgot about it. I know that sounds strange but I actually put it out of my mind at some point, and just went to bed. In the morning the guy was gone.

Dan had a new pair of boots that were scuffed on the tops.

"Nice boots." I said. "Thanks, I found em." He replied.

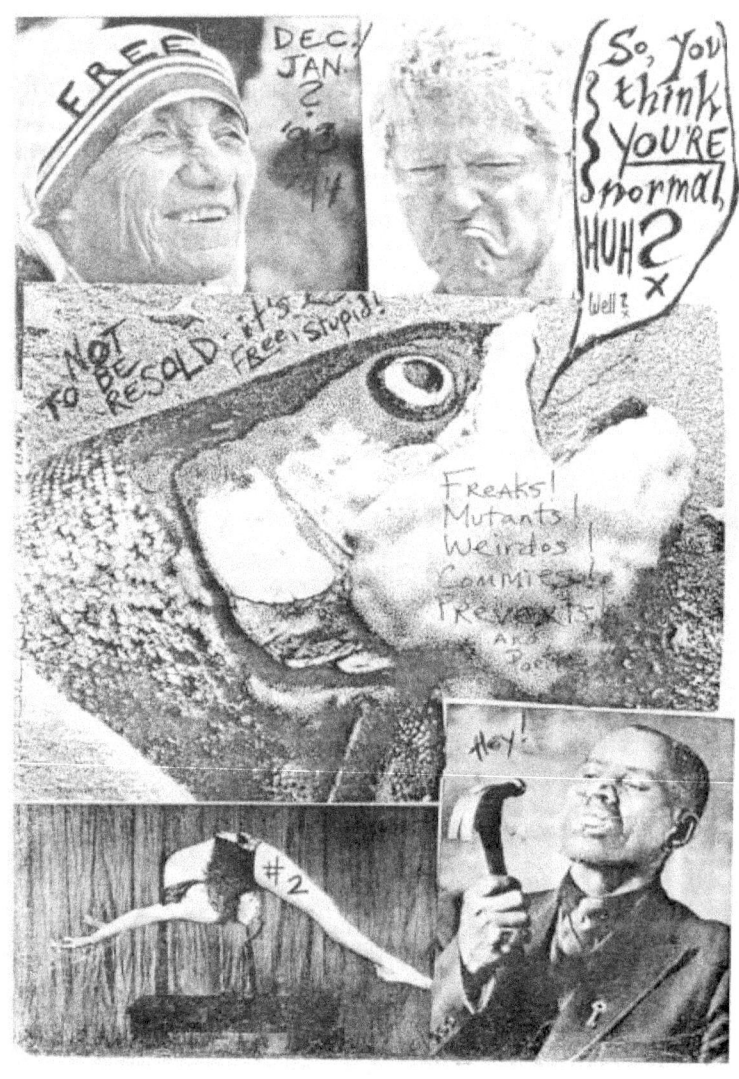

SYTYN

When I was much, much younger I lived in a second-floor apartment across from a gay bookstore in Philadelphia for a while. (Thanks to them for introducing me to Hothead Paisan at such an impressionable age, by the way.) It was a decent apartment, with a nice fireplace. We had several cats, my girlfriend and I. I owned an ancient underwood typewriter, which I place on a board in the window, I drank a lot of coffee and smoked way too much. And on rainy spring nights I'd sit in the window watching the people go in and out of the bookstore, and I'd try to write...poetry. This was before tattooing, before the west coast, before the zine, before I squatted, before I dropped out of civilization for the wild years. This was the start of that. It was the BEFORE TIMES.

It was horrible, in retrospect. But at the time I felt like it was a way to recognize that inside me hides an angry intellectual snob, someone who could rise above living in shitsville, who'd worked in factories. Some kind of Henry Miller/Bukowski/Hemingway persona. Some kind of talent that made me better than what I'd come from. I hadn't started working at art in earnest yet, collage and a few drawings or paintings were all I'd done, so writing seemed a natural outlet for me instead.

I'd listen to really scratchy jazz records, 78s, or I'd listen to crappy local punk rock. No difference really, to me. I'd smoke too much and stare out the window, looking at the streetlights on the pavement, and try to put words together and make poems. I sucked at it. I hadn't read a lot of poetry- just cummings, Bukowski, and a few others. I never enjoyed reading poetry and still don't. In my english classes I'd always dreaded the poetry section, having to distill something pointless and plotless into a meaning...trying to read between lines. It never suited me but, I was styling myself as a writer, and instead of trying to write stories, or something that had a real narrative, or something challenging…

I was going to write poetry, because it didn't have to make any real sense.

It was an awful and embarrassing period of my life and to this day I look back on myself, sitting in that window, with distress and shame.

Shortly after starting this madness, I signed up for a group which would read their writing to each other, like a mutual critique society kind of thing. I never read my own work, since I only went once. The middle-aged woman reading her memoir, the fat balding new age guy who had a novel he'd written (firmly falling into the man-romance genre) … these were not my people.

I went home and started writing about how stupid the laundromat near my house was, and doing more cut and paste things until eventually I had twenty pages of crap. Then I photocopied it with a stolen kinko's cartridge and handed it out to some friends. I kept that zine going for about two years, maybe three. I was proud of it and actually, even now, I think I did a decent job. It was much better than silky fingers of glistening rain, or whatever that other shit was all about.

So if you've done something embarrassing creatively, the best thing to do is burn the evidence and make a zine for a few years. Just talk about stuff you hate, stuff you like. It doesn't have to be great as long as it's not pretentious and completely fake.

I think in some ways this is just the reincarnation of that zine.

west texas trouble

I was on a cross-country road trip, with a colleague. We were driving through west texas, on a major highway. In the area where we were, even the major highway was pretty desolate. There had been a truck stop or gas station about every hundred miles, and every one of them was solitary with no other buildings in sight.

These weren't really towns, the exits, just places to get more gas to get to the next gas station.

It was pretty late at night, and she had been driving for like four hours. I usually can drive for about eight before I'm tired out (I go on frequent road trips) but she could only manage four or five before it was "my turn" again. We were also getting low on gas, at about a quarter tank, and you learn from road travel to fill up when you get the chance. So she was looking for a gas station as we drove along.

It's really corny but we were talking about fate, and destiny, and some other weird shit at the time. That kind of conversation gets me keyed up and worried, so I was trying to change the subject. She took an exit while we were talking, and I got out my coffee mug so I could fill up for my turn driving. We pulled into a typical nowhereville gas station- just the station and a trailer out back (I assume thinking back it was probably where the people who owned it lived). There was another car parked in front of the doors off to one side.

We got out, still talking, and walked up to the double doors, each of us grabbing a door handle.

The doors were locked. I turned and looked around to see if there was a sign (sometimes places will put up a "back in 5 minutes") and noticed several things in succession; the coffeemaker in side was half-way done brewing a fresh pot of coffee, the monitors that showed the store were visible from outside, where we were, but all of them were showing static, and there was a splash of bright red on the door in the back of the place, which was closed. I suddenly realized I was looking at a huge streak of blood, with handprints in it.

Every hair on my neck stood up. My friend began shaking the door, yelling "WE NEED TO GET GAS" but I had already turned and walked away from the doors.

"We have to LEAVE. NOW" I grabbed her arm and started propelling her back to the car. Now I noticed the other car in the lot. It had no plates. It was dingy and had dents. There was an empty gun rack in the window of it. I ran to the car, dragging her with me. She seemed to take forever to open her door and get in (she had the keys still)

The whole time she kept saying, but we need gas! while I tried to explain to her, "there's BLOOD in there. BLOOD."

after what seemed like a year she pulled the car out. when we were backing up, I saw through the windows that the back door in the gas station was opening. We had pulled away before anyone came out, thankfully.

I freaked out until we were twenty miles down the highway. I tried to call police but had no signal, I didn't get a phone signal until we had driven about forty miles and got to a truck stop. again, not in a town, just a building on its own in the middle of nothingness.

I called the cops, they thanked me, and I never heard anything more about it. To this day I feel like if I hadn't freaked out, we probably would have met the robber- or whoever was in the back room of the place.

I also wish I had been able to find out what the hell had happened there. It was a Chevron station, somewhere in the western part of TX (at least, within about a hundred miles or so of the signs for those places, on RT 10)

squalorous hoarding.

How do you come back from being a hoarder, packrat, filthy slob, pig, messie, messmaker, disorganizer, whirlwind, crusty, squatter, punkrock junkyard maven???

THROW ALMOST EVERYTHING AWAY.

Also moving into a nicer house which is not in so much disrepair is a good idea. My last house I rented was dismally under-maintained before I arrived- carpets coated in cat urine, walls in grease. Holes in the walls, cracks running top to bottom, water heaters that hardly worked, leaks, cracks, windows that never closed, no baseboards, and more…

The new place is not the hilton but DAMN is it a ton nicer in comparison. The owner takes care of the place. The floors are clean. The walls are bright and happy. I have hot running water at all times. And the rent? NOT ALL THAT MUCH HIGHER.

Also. I got rid of a bunch of things, moving in. So I now have more space. I have less piles. I am not all the way unpacked but I am really close to it and it feels GREAT. My house is so much calmer, this place is so much better. I'm content.

I used to really have a major problem with hoarding. I lived in very squalorous conditions again and again. Part of it was, yeah, slumlords and poverty- but the rest was ME. I struggle with maintaining my little bit of new order every day. It's really difficult sometimes but I know that the minute I let up on it I will be back to level 3 mayhem and chaos very quickly. It added a lot to my depression, it made life harder for me than it needed to be, but getting out from under is really not as easy as just getting rid of stuff. There's a lot of mental squalor to deal with too and that is way more difficult.

From years of having nothing I learned to hoard. I learned that if I had something that meant something to me it might go away…

My parents had me really young. My mom tried her best but I think that taking my things away when I misbehaved was a bad choice; I don't think that she had malice in doing this but man did it ever have repercussions for me in my adult life. I've had to re-learn to cherish and maintain my belongings, to think of them as MINE and not as temporary…to take care of the things I own instead of viewing that as pointless because anything could be taken away, be gone, at any time.

My mom didn't grow up rich herself so I do not blame her or think that she knew any better. Man I am a decade or more older than she was when she was raising me and I still wouldn't do half as well as she did…but this one thing, above all, changed the way I live, and I still fight with it, still try to stay conscious of it, still am learning that objects and tools and belongings can have meaning and can be kept under control.

For me that is the root of my squalor and hoarding.

Years after that I was broke all the time- I needed many things and didn't have them. So I got into the habit of taking what I could when I could get it and saving things for later. not always the best habit, when it gets out of hand. Thrift is fine but there are limits.

I'm a member at squalorsurvivors and I found some of the ways they support each other to be really helpful to me when I was trying to start changing this. Taking pictures of a messy area showed me a lot; there's a tendency to just stop seeing a mess that you see every day, the way a pair of tinted sunglasses soon loses its color effect...it becomes something that you are inured to and can no longer see with your own eyes. So photographs helped me a lot.

Also techniques like starting with ONE thing. Just one. Not cleaning a room but cleaning off a small area in a room. The notion that I should let others into my environment to see it as motivation. Asking others for help...just even talking about it.

All of it helped.

I've talked about this a tiny bit here but not in so much depth I don't think. I mean now they have like "hoarders" on tv...and I see a lot on the internet about it...but really it's hard to admit to and hard to come out of. I find people that allow the cameras in really brave, regardless of the result. There's an underlying terror to living in squalor- that someone will knock at the door. I still have the startle reaction to a knock on my door but I am trying to overcome that, more and more all the time.

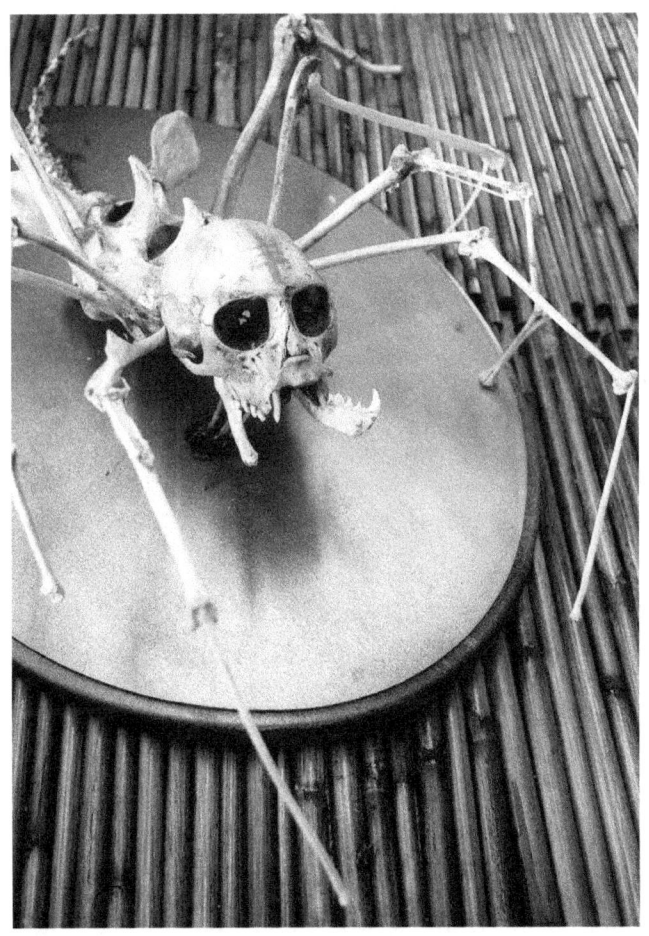

the creatures.

I moved into a house in the woods, part of an old ranger station, about a year ago. It's sincerely in the middle of nowhere, dark as shit at night, and surrounded by the kind of old pine and fir woods that only Oregon can grow. I at first was ecstatic- I even was willing to pay the high rent. I'm an artist, a professional artist, and the place is wonderful. Huge, south-facing windows, high on a hill over a river for a grand view; the front room is one large space, about 1500 square feet, and attached is a bedroom, kitchen, and bath. It's basically the dream studio, only instead of being stuck in a hellish noise-hole of a city, it's in the beautiful, dark, mossy woods.

I have only one neighbor. She is unintrusive, normal, and boring. She has chickens.

I moved in in a state of grace. My art area takes up the entire front room with the exception of a small corner for a couch and TV (I watch a lot of VHS but don't have cable). The front wall, with the huge windows, is lined now with my desks and tables, on which I store all my gear.

I work in a lot of mediums; I've done photography, paint in oils, watercolor, and in the last year or two I've begun doing sculptures. Now my sculpted work is not "sculpted", more of "assemblage", since I rarely use clay. I collect and build mounts, plaques, which combine animal remains and paint, feathers, wood, and carved pieces into totems of a sort. I've had two damn successful shows of this kind of stuff, and the only trouble I've had has been doing enough research to avoid using any illegal materials (songbirds and whales and such) in my work.

I intended to continue mining this rich vein of inspiration in my new work space, and felt for the forest few months that being so isolated was even helping me to gain more inspiration. Having the woods, sea, and river so close has been a boon for my collection of "supplies"; and my eye has been more honed by this constant exposure to nature than it was before (I had previously been living in town, and then on a farm in a rural town.) I have always found isolation to be best for my work, but here I experience a more profound aloneness, and I still, despite everything, enjoy it.

It was in July, on return from a long vacation, that I began to have the dreams. I would wake up suddenly, my heart pounding. I felt a complete loathing, as if a slug had touched my tongue. I did not at first remember the dreams, but as this summer wore on they began to sneak through during the day, in fragments, slight jolts of memory here and there. I'd be pouring coffee in the morning, staring out the window at the trees, and shudder. I'd hear a tapping sound of a branch and cringe.

Once, I walked through a spiderweb and almost vomited from fear- there seemed to be no reason for any of it.

And yes- I'm an eccentric artist. I've suffered from extreme depression at times in my life and am all too familiar with the sensations of delusion and madness. I spent many of my younger years drugged, drunk, and hollering or fighting. I know that my ability to convince any authority of my honesty is simply feeble. So I haven't spoken of this, at all. Not to anyone but you.

I should say that my work entails having a lot of creepy items in my studio. My studio which is in my house. I get a lot of strange animal remains from various friends and clients in sundry stages of decay or dissolution and sometimes from questionable sources.

Right before I began having these dreams, a friend of mine had returned from a trip to northern Africa, to a nation in some disarray, from a trip to promote literacy. (she is a volunteer) She brought me, on her return, a pair of monkey skulls. one was complete, female, and small. A vervet or something, perfectly legal and not too unusual. The other appeared to be a male, slightly larger, and with the back of its head cut out crudely. "Bushmeat." she said. "They eat their brains. It's legal, it came through customs fine and all and isn't CITES, but I have no idea what it actually is."

As the dreams progressed, and began to make themselves more known to me, I decided to build something with the monkey skulls. At first I placed them on a mount with some veves, voodoo charm symbolism. I chose papa legba (a protector spirit of sorts) as their totem. I used red silk and various other items to assemble a mount for an artwork. I was satisfied when finished, but on waking I felt it was the wrong use. and I began to pick through bird and cat bones, a bin of which I have amassed over the year just passed. I lay out a handful of bones and suddenly the shape came to me in a flash as if I remembered it instead of imagining it. And I knew somehow it was from my dreams. I ended up abandoning my other work in order to finish this piece as quickly and well as possible. It came together with almost no effort; simply looking I knew which bone to apply where.

And I found myself not building a totem, but a golem.

I spent three days working, drinking coffee, no sleep or food. The staining and painting took the longest, and while drying I would pace the room. I felt almost frenzied. As I finished, and mounted it to its plaque, I broke off one of the fore-legs. I cursed, reattached it, and finally, happily, went to bed.

In the morning it was no longer straight on its mount. I decided the glue must have been still tacky, and that it shifted of its own weight. But my dreams had been horrible. I'd seen it trying to get off the mount, straining like a fly on sticky paper. its foreleg reached out to me and pried at my lips, trying to get in. I added more glue, all round.

Over the next few nights, my dreams became more vivid. The creature was on the ceiling, dropping down on a thick wire of silk, reaching for me. It was in the shower, weaving in a corner. Its jaws (which I had lovingly chosen, skunk's jaws to be exact) gnashed and slobber fell off in pats like butter. If I closed my eyes I saw it. Creeping. It could move fast. Then one night I snapped. I have a habit of napping on the couch in my studio.

The creature had been hanging on its plaque on the wall. Each morning it seemed slightly off from the position of the night before- but I attributed this to the glue still not set (a week later...the mind is so clever, isn't it?) That night- I had been drawing. I have a few commissions that at that time I was still maintaining some little interest in completing. I grew tired, and as had become my habit, I lay on the couch; at this point I always turned my back to the wall where the creature hangs. Right now as I type it is to my left, clutching its plaque, waiting for me to see it again. To be honest I cannot stand to look at it. I lay on the couch and dozed. I dreamed that the creature poised itself over my face- it brushed my lips apart and inserted one leg, then another. finally it deposited something sticky on my tongue- and yes, if your mind went there, that was exactly what it was like. I'm a woman, I like men- I know that taste and feel. It was awful. I woke up flinging my arms to my face and could still taste it, faintly.

I looked at the plaque and- the creature was just settling itself. It seriously looked- well have you ever tossed something onto a bouncy bed, and seen that last tiny bounce before it stops? it was that sort of motion.

I left my house. I live, as I said in the woods. Being outdoors here isn't safe-feeling, exactly. I mean, there are bear, cougars. It's pitch dark and ancient. I wasn't happy about being outside but I was even less willing to stay indoors.

I had an epiphany. I could not keep this thing.

I could not keep this thing, this child of mine, in my studio. In my home.

I sat on my porch for a very long time. I soon forgot the darkness and the lateness- and I thought of someone-

I would give the creature to him. It would fit his collection perfectly. I can't, even now, imagine being PAID for this thing. Yet, I felt, the act of giving it to someone would transfer its- affections- interest- to them instead of me.

Or perhaps it would do nothing once it was away from me, from this place.

when I ventured back inside, it was still. inanimate. The feeling I had had of it being live, in motion arrested- that feeling was gone. I lay down, breathed a deep sigh, and slept.

This time, I dreamed I was outdoors. where I had just sat on the porch, in the dim light from the door's window. Over my porch hangs, very high above, the long branches of a douglas fir. My attention was drawn there by cones falling to the ground in front of me. I looked up and saw, lit only by starlight, a dark shape. It screeched; I screamed. It dove at me and in absolutely irrational dream logic I saw it, even in the tarry blackness. I saw its feet, its face.

I'd call it a harpy but it wasn't; any more than the first creature was a "spidermonkey".

As I ran from it a long form on the ground pursued me. I only got a glimpse of it; I feel that it is next in line. I began assembling immediately upon waking; this happened last night and I am here typing as the first set of articulations, the first layer of glue, begins to dry in front of me, and I plan to finish this and gift it before I sleep again. I've also, for some reason, began to lay out another set of bones- long, curving spine and short claws.

I have to go brew more coffee. I can't work on it any longer and I MUST sleep now so that I can wake up tonight to finish. I can't prop it upright yet but I can explain where I'm at so far. Still need to assemble the ribs, sternum, and jaws. It's getting closer, though. It's starting to look- familiar.

Not entirely pleasant now that the head is attached, and I wish I'd not given it its hands until the end. what's done is done, though.

I woke up with my arms behind my back, like they'd been handcuffed, both arms tingling and sore from bloodlack. I feel queasy. I woke up lying on my back, my head tilted up, all the way up. I can barely look forward normally right now to type this; the strain on my neck is incredible, I've at least got a bad muscle spasm and at worst a strain or sprain.

I'm going to take a few ibuprofen and then come back and tell the dream. I've got coffee brewing and I foresee a long night ahead of construction. I finished attaching some more pieces. I spent a few hours tinkering with angles and placements and wires, then fell onto the couch for a nap.

I felt fairly safe; after all, I'd told the story, decided to gift these creatures rather than keep or sell them, and this one wasn't quite as animate, yet, as the last. I cannot remember the whole dream, only I know it was long. One of those neverending dreams with repetitive elements that frustrate.

I do remember the end, though. I was walking, on a path. From above I was suddenly grabbed and my arms thrust behind me. Then I was lifted, by my arms, from the ground. It was excruciating and as I was lifted something sharp began to grab and tear at my hair. I was unable to struggle against my own weight, and screamed.

i woke up as I described, lying on my back with my arms beneath me. My arms were asleep and tingling and my hair was in clumps on the pillow. The "harpy" had settled a bit on the perch when I finally was able to bring myself to look at it.

I'll be working straight through, now, I think.

There's something outside.

I have huge front windows, my work table faces one. I know for someone who spends a lot of time watching horror movies, it may seem odd but I prefer being able to see out of the windows, rather than having curtains up. And there is something out there, slinking around in the bushes. It's long.

The neighbor left me a note today while I was napping. "Two of my hens are gone, keep an eye on your cat, maybe a owl out here" Whatever is moving around outside is in the bushes by the drive, which leads to her house.

I suppose it could be a cougar. I keep glancing out the window while I work. I wish I could work faster. I wish I could finish both of these pieces at once, tonight, now.

I've made plans to meet my friend to give him his gift. I haven't described it to him at all, just told him it was something I made just for him, for his collection. He's coming by in an hour or so.

That went...less than well. I handed it over willingly- if there were to be no consequences, he will truly value the thing. But as he took it a weight lifted from me. I saw him to his car and I knew it no longer wanted me, but him. Back to work.

He should have been home by now, it's been three hours. His wife left a message here too, that he isn't answering his phone. I have a sinking feeling, I know what's happened. He's been assaulted by it. I regret giving it to him now- he was so happy to have it, so excited.

and there's the matter of the "harpy", too.

I don't know who it belongs to yet.

I'm finished with her.

I think I know who should have her. Who she will enjoy.

A collector I know.

I can't find my cat. The litterbox is full of what look like owl pellets.

I called the collector. She arrived fresh as a daisy, and glad to have something for her macabre collection. She's eyed my work at every opening so far, and was flattered that I gave this to her. She almost couldn't believe her luck. That was this afternoon. I still haven't heard from her, or the other artist who I gave the spider to. It's now evening. Perhaps it's a coincidence that they've both gone missing. I know it isn't, though. I can't keep denying this.

I keep thinking about the next creature- its bones are already laid out in order here on a piece of canvas. It won't fit on the table so I lay it out on the floor. I don't feel right about it.

I mean, these other two, I can rationalize giving them away. I can pretend to myself that they won't attack their owners- they're after ME, right? nobody else?

But I know this isn't true. And this bigger one has a more malevolent feeling, a more intentional feeling. The first one- well, I was just building from a model I saw in dreams, right? I couldn't know that it was animate. That it WANTED to be built. But building this last one, I know. I know before I even start, that I am building art to destroy someone with.

and I wish I could not know that. Or turn off my conscience somehow, and not care. I want to resist. I don't want to use my hands for this kind of work. What am I going to do? Can I kill it? Does that mean I have to kill all three?

Because despite everything, I feel the same fondness for these two that i do for any piece of art I have made that I am satisfied with.

Am I really evil enough to value my own art over the life of a person?

I think I'm going to fight it. I have a revolver. I don't think that will work, though.

vegan placenta?

So, the big question isn't why you do it. Isn't "what does tofu taste like, styrofoam or paper?". It isn't how you manage.

The big question is, is placenta vegan?

I mean, really. I am speaking to those who are the "ethical" vegan type. Who don't participate in the ritualized factory farming system which tortures then kills wee creatures. To the morrisey kids. It's the death, suffering, and hate you're trying to keep out of your diet, right? So...

Placenta.

It's produced by a joyful moment. It doesn't hurt. It kills nothing. It isn't dead. It also could be naturally produced by free roaming creatures. It is a simple side effect of what some would refer to as "a little miracle bundle from god".

To take it a step further, let's say my acreage has some wild cattle. I notice one is having a calf and I run to help, and then the calf is born and the placenta comes out and the cow and child wander away to continue living freely in cow heaven (...could they actually survive without people? Or would they starve like they do in India? That's another story.) My question is, can I eat that placenta? If I'm vegan?

Can I eat a section of leg that my friend has cut off of himself, and offered to me? Can I cannibalize someone who is willing?

Or, is it just that it is an animal product? Is that the reason? Because I know from growing up in farmland that without animal waste there's no plants. Fertilizer. So...ALL food that is grown organically uses animal waste fertilizer. This means that the carrots we eat are grown only by using animals and their products to nurture them. Meaning that big farms rely on factory farmed animal wastes in order to grow. Meaning that even if it's local, organic, etc, some animal somewhere was robbed of its precious fewmets to make food for you to eat, which means it was confined, so that the fewmets could be obtained. Which kind of rubs me wrong in the logic center when I start thinking about this stuff.

I have very vague notions about all this. It somehow feels wrong to me. But I've eaten placenta and it wasn't very good. So if it's just a matter of taste, I can understand.

And what about my friend's thigh slice? I need to know. That one just seems, well, difficult. If it's freely offered? Hmmm. (I would eat it anyway, but I'm not vegan. I'm fruitarian.)

legal cannibalism.

I am a legal, humane cannibal. I've had a lot of people asking me questions about that, so I figured I would answer some here in the blog, in case others were wondering.

I have drawn and painted portraits of many cannibals. I find it fascinating that this taboo is so strong, and somewhat confusing- our taboo against murder is less strong than this. (In western society)

Q:Why?

A: It started as an in-joke among a few of my friends and I. I was watching the movie "Alive", and complaining throughout the documentary attached to the DVD that they not once asked them about the taste.

Then a friend had a section of thigh muscle removed, and brought it to me, frozen, as a challenge. "You want to find out, go ahead and find out," he said. So- I did. I cooked it and ate it.

Someone else brought me their removed earlobes. I cooked and ate them.

Then, I sat in on a friend getting skin removal done (scarification). she bagged up this hunk of her skin and handed it to me.

This happened a few more times, and as of now I have had six or so people give me bits of themselves to eat. It was mainly curiosity at first, and still is. I wanted to know if it would change me, make me a wendigo, give me laughing sickness, make me strong, or just be...meat like any other meat.

Q: didn't you get grossed out?

A: Yeah, the first time was weird. Right before I took the first bite I felt freaked out. Nervous and kind of grossed out.

I sort of forced myself to think "pork chop" and took that bite, and then after that it was easy.

Q: You're a cannibal.

A: You didn't ask a question.

Q: Isn't that illegal?

A: No. Nobody was harmed. I did not do surgery on anyone; their flesh is theirs to do what they want with. None of this was done illegally in any way, nor is any of it inhumane. Actually, it's the closest you could probably get to ethically-sourced meat. The source being capable of consent, alive, and willing.

Q: What about diseases? KURU. Mad cow!

A: I have never eaten brains or spinal tissue. And everything I've eaten has been thoroughly cooked.

Q: But…WHY?

A: I had to know. I had the opportunity to try something that would not harm anyone, and so I decided that life is short and I should try anything I can that is not going to harm someone. So, I did. I also feel like it's a very rare opportunity, and that not taking it was somehow the wrong thing to do.

TRUE CRIMES

Biography of Ed Kemper.

Ed Kemper was a large man. He spent most of his life in very small spaces.

He was, unlike many killers, more than willing to openly discuss both his crimes and his feelings about them. Unlike most, he did not pretend to innocence or argue his liability. He also spoke freely about the urges he felt, and their origins.

"When I see a pretty girl walking down the street, I think two things: one part of me wants to take her home, be real nice and treat her right; the other part wonders what her head would look like on a stick."

He was fifteen when he killed his grandparents. He said that he had killed his grandmother "to see what it felt like"; also, he was angry at them because they had taken away his rifle. Most killers will try to justify a crime, by giving reasons they think anyone might have done it. Kemper quite openly admitted that curiosity about killing, and simple anger, were his main reasons for the killing. He then killed his grandfather, as well, most likely to prevent retribution or further punishment. It was also a way for him to leave the living situation, as he disliked living with them.

"...my grandmother who thought she had more balls than any man and was constantly emasculating me and my grandfather to prove it. I couldn't please her. It was like being in jail. I became a walking time bomb and I finally blew. "

He was imprisoned for these killings until he was 21. During his confinement, he was diagnosed paranoid schizophrenic and tested with a fairly high IQ. He was an intelligent person- but his mind was a bit broken. Whether the diagnosis of PS was accurate or not (diagnostics at that time did not recognize sociopathy or ASPD as proper diagnoses) could be questioned. (He is currently being treated for paranoid schizophrenia.)

He went to live with his mother when he was released.

This was probably a bad idea.

"I can't get away from her. She knows all my buttons and I dance like a puppet."

His history with his mother was dark. She most likely suffered from borderline personality disorder. Many sociopaths and killers have had parents who have suffered from this disorder. The instability, rages, and unpredictable behavior it causes tend to make childhood very difficult for their children. Whether or not Kemper was born with a tendency to murder, his upbringing with this mother could only have exacerbated it, and brought it to the surface.

She previously had made him stay in the low-ceilinged basement because she believed he might rape or attack his sisters. Whether or not she was correct about this is lost to history- it is possible that Kemper was in fact menacing and perhaps violent or overtly sexual in his interactions with them. Given his personality, her fears may have been justified- he describes torturing cats and other animals openly during his youth, which might make anyone squeamish. Their relationship was obviously troubled, either way, and her abuse of him, combined with his own dark personality, made a very dangerous combination.

Three years after he was released, he began to kill women.

"Alive, they were distant, not sharing with me. I was trying to establish a relationship, and there was no relationship... When they were being killed, there wasn't anything going on in my mind except that they were going to be mine... That was the only way they could be mine."

He was an opportunist, picking up hitchhikers and strangling or shooting them. He found their dead bodies fascinating and spent time with their remains, dismembering them, saving parts, and having sex with the corpses. He kept many trophies and body parts in his room at home, including heads and hands. He sliced bits of meat from their legs, to cook and eat later in macaroni casserole (he was apparently not a gourmet.) For a while, he carried teeth, and hair from his victims to remember them. He buried the head of one of his victims just outside his window, facing him so that he could speak with her at night.

"They were like spirit wives... I still had their spirits. I still have them."

Eventually, he killed his mother as well. Her borderline disorder caused her to be contentious and violently emotional, and to engage in long rages during which the two would argue repetitively.

"My mother and I started right in on horrendous battles, just horrible battles, violent and vicious. I've never seen such a vicious verbal battle with anyone. It would go to fists with a man, but this was my mother, and I couldn't stand the thought of my mother and I doing these things. She insisted on it, and just over stupid things. I remember one roof-raiser was over whether I should have my teeth cleaned"

Kemper waited until his mother slept, then bashed her head with a claw hammer until she was dead. He decapitated her, removing her vocal cords along the way. He threw her larynx into the garbage disposal. He had sex with her head. He set it up afterwards, propped across the room, and used it as a dartboard. He played with her body for hours. When he grew tired of her, he called her friend and invited her over for dinner. When the woman arrived, he attacked her, clubbed her then strangled her. He also decapitated her, placing her body in his bed. He then rested in his mother's bed for a while.

"her head...I put it on a shelf and screamed at it for an hour... threw darts at it... smashed her face in...It was so hard. I cut off her head, and I humiliated her, of course. She was dead, because of the way she raised her son."

However after these two killings he fled. Unlike most killers Kemper was very direct about his circumstances. He knew that unlike his previous killings, he would be caught for these. He had killed his mother in a fit of temper, not with premeditated lust, so he had not been cautious. He called the police, some of whom were personal friends of his, and turned himself in.

"I can't get it out of my mind. It got heavier and heavier, and harder and harder, and I drank more and more, and I came close to blowing it every time I'd drink too much. I don't mean doing something crazy, but almost giving myself away. The farther along I went, you'll have to agree, the sloppier I got and the more careless I got, both in picking girls up, taking chances, and not following my set rules, and also in disposal of the evidence."

He spoke freely about his work. His confession, like the writings of Sagawa, are detailed and complex. He discussed his motivations and his emotions during the killings and did not shy from describing his own fears and inadequacies.

"I had fantasies about mass murder, whole groups of select women I could get together in one place, get them dead and then make mad passionate love to their dead corpses. Taking life away from them, a living human being, and then having possession of everything that used to be theirs. All that would be mine. Everything."

Kemper again was unusual in that he requested the death penalty and was denied. Many serial killers attempt to draw out the judicial process and avoid the death penalty, but Kemper was disappointed that he was denied execution.

Ed Kemper is currently among the general population in the California Medical Facility in Vacaville, California, and has another parole hearing in 2012.

"You haven't asked the questions I expected a reporter to ask. Oh, what is it like to have sex with a dead body? What does it feel like to sit on your living room couch and look over and see two decapitated girls' heads on the arm of the couch? The first time, it makes you sick to your stomach."

Biography of Carl Panzram, with apologies.

"I was so full of hate that there was no room in me for such feelings as love, pity, kindness or honor or decency."

Carl Panzram was born at an odd time in American history. In 1891, in rural Minnesota, he was born into a poor farming family. His father left the family when he was 7. Brought up in an atmosphere of swift and merciless punishment, and unending toil for little or no reward, Panzram learned early that the world most likely hated him, or at best was indifferent.

Unlike most in this situation, he decided to return hate with hate, and indifference to suffering with callous disregard.

"The older I got the meaner I got."

The nation, in Panzram's youth, was suddenly much easier to traverse. He was one of the first traveling killers. Canneries, industry, and labor disputes were common during his lifetime- the fact that child labor was being seriously defended by those in authority at that time did much to warp his perspective. He began his violence very young, and at the age of eight, fighting and attacking other children. He was sent to a reform school at eleven. Reform schools and prisons at that time were not dedicated to rehabilitation- punishment was the purpose, and Panzram experienced several years of sodomy, beatings, forced labor, and starvation.

When he was released, he was primed and ready to take revenge on the world.

"I first began to think that I was being unjustly imposed upon. Then I began to hate those who abused me. Then I began to think that I would have my revenge just as soon and as often as I could injure someone else. Anyone at all would do."

In 1906, after another failed attempt at reform school, Panzram hopped a train out into the world.

"I fully decided when I left there just how I would live my life. I made up my mind that I would rob, burn, destroy and kill everywhere I went and everybody I could as long as I lived."

He was almost immediately arrested for burglary and imprisoned again. At the age of 14, he was fully grown, man-size. He was able to escape, and began burning churches as a hobby along his travels. His fierce hatred for religion had been beaten into him during his time at the christian reform schools. He had begun to rape anyone and everyone he came across that was vulnerable; his anger was not limited by gender or age.

Panzram changed his name during this time, and wandered west again. He eventually enlisted in the military; he was court-martialed and sentenced again, almost immediately, for burglary. He was sent to the federal penitentiary at Fort Leavenworth- an old, brutally-managed prison. He was treated as an adult, since it was not known that he was only 16 at the time. A code of silence was strictly enforced there, solitary confinement and whipping were the chosen punishments. He was there for four years- breaking rocks for ten hours a day, every day. when he left he was stronger and angrier than before.

I've found that I simply can't do Panzram justice. His ability to express himself, and the sheer amount of information in existence chronicling his life, are overwhelming to me. He is a nihilist inspiration;

he was the epitome of misanthropic, all-encompassing-hateful badassery, and his story is told very well and with thorough attention to detail here. You can also, like I did, buy his autobiography, which he wrote while in prison.

I hate to be a quitter but I honestly feel that my writing ability has broken under the weight of detail available about his life. Sorry about that.

Biography of Arwin Meiwes.

Arwin Meiwes posted internet ads asking for a well-built, fair-complected male to volunteer to be eaten by him. Seriously, he was seeking a cannibal mate. He repeatedly attempted to meet someone who would fulfill his fantasy, but the men he met tended to be less than serious, and many would not meet him in real life. "I hope you can come quick to me, I am a hungry cannibal. Please tell me your height and weight and I will butcher and eat your fine flesh."

He spoke, in fact, to hundreds of men until finally, in 2001, Bernd-Jurgen Brandes responded to him, "You don't have to buy meat again, there will be plenty left.", and the two met in person shortly afterward. Meiwes said,"I had the fantasy, and in the end I fulfilled it."

The two went to Meiwes' home, where he sliced off Brandes' penis, and cooked it. They ate it together, recording everything on video. Then, at Brandes' request, he stabbed Brandes in the neck repeatedly, killing him. He then butchered the body and consumed it. Meiwes says, "My friend enjoyed dying, death. I only waited horrified for the end after doing the deed. It took so terribly long."

Meiwes expressed disappointment in his partner, saying "The next one must be young but not so fat."

He kept about 60 pounds of the meat in his refrigerator, eating it over a span of time, saving it and relishing it, cooking it with cabbage and potatoes. He labeled the packages of human flesh "schnitzels". He was caught when he placed another ad. A young man noticed it, and reported it to the police. He was tried and first sentenced to 8 years, but public outcry soon called for a second trial, and he was given life in prison.

His defense was that the death was consensual, and could not be considered murder. According to some involved in the case, the video tape made by the participants made this a very strong defense. The fact that cannibalism is itself not a crime in Germany, made his case even stronger.

Meiwes was convicted of manslaughter and sentenced to 8 and a half years in prison in 2004; the case attracted considerable media attention and also led to a debate over whether Meiwes could be convicted at all given that Brandes had voluntarily and knowingly participated in the act. Evidence provided by the defense was a video tape made my Meiwes of the entire incident.

During the trial Meiwes' lawyer, Harald Ermel, cited e-mails in which the victim insisted on being killed and eaten. One read: "There's absolutely no way back for me, only forwards, through your teeth."

Meiwes' video of the killing in March 2001, as well as a note left by Bandes in his apartment saying he was a willing victim, persuaded even prosecutors to concede the death was voluntary.

Media and observers were kept outside while the tape was shown to the court. One newspaper said a woman almost fainted during the film, which shows Meiwes talking to the severed head while he disembowels the body, hung from a hook.

Biography of Issei Sagawa.

Issei Sagawa was a Japanese man, who was studying at Censier Institute in Paris. There he met a young woman named Renee Hartevelt, with whom he became friendly.

On June 11, 1981, she went to visit him at his home. He gave her some whiskey in a cup of tea, and made it clear that he was interested in her. She rebuffed him. As she was reading, he shot her in the back of the head with a .22 caliber rifle. Sagawa said "I was surprised how quiet she was, and tried to clean up the blood but gave up."

He disrobed her, cut off part of her left breast and a piece of her nose, and ate them. He chewed off a piece of her buttock and ate it. He said "[It] melted in my mouth like raw tuna in a sushi restaurant."

He photographed her corpse, had sex with it, and cut it up into slices. For the next day he snuggled up to her and ate parts of her body, until the flies arrived. Then he cut her body into smaller pieces and packed her into a suitcase set, and called a cab. He left the suitcases in a park and returned home, and continued to eat the slices he had saved for the next day, until he was arrested.

Now the story gets really interesting.

He was arrested in France, and sentenced to a mental health facility. His father, a prominent and quite rich man, arranged for Issei to be transferred to the Matsuzawa psychiatric hospital in Japan instead.

This was done, and when Issei arrived he was pronounced sane and released. Issei Sagawa, being rich, was able to walk free within less than five years of killing, raping, and dismembering and eating a young woman. He was able also to obtain a passport from Japan and travel to Germany and other places.

He is currently a kind of macabre celebrity in Japan. He has appeared on talk shows, in porn, and has written several (fairly crappy) films, one of which discusses his feelings about the murder. He brags openly about having enjoyed eating Renee. He has also been interviewed for several magazines. For a while he had a personal site up containing his statement about the crime, but it has since disappeared. He occasionally produces paintings for sale as well.

Issei's statement about his crime:

I am amazed. She's the most beautiful woman I've ever seen. Tall, blonde, with pure white skin, she astonishes me with her grace. I invited her to my home for a Japanese dinner. She accepts. After the meal I asked her to read my favorite German Expressionist poem. As she reads i can't keep my eyes off her. After she leaves I can still smell her body on the bed sheet where she sat reading the poem. I lick the chopsticks and dishes she used. I can taste her lips. My passion is so great. I want to eat her. If I do she will be mine forever. There is no escape from this desire. I arrange for her to read the poem for me once more. I lie to her. I tell her I want to record the poem on tape for my Japanese teacher. She believes. I prepare everything. The cassette recorder for the poem, the rifle for the sacrifice. She arrives on time. After drinking tea and whiskey, she speaks. She smiles at me. But I know inside that I'm the strangest one of all. Her yellow sleeveless top shows off her beautiful white arms.

I turn on the recorder. She starts to read . She speaks in perfect German. I reach for the rifle hidden beside the chest of drawers. I stand slowly and aim the riffle at the back of her head. I cannot stop myself. There is a loud sound and her body falls from the chair onto the floor. It is like she is watching me. I see her cheeks, her eyes, her nose and mouth, the blood pouring from her head. I try to talk to her, but she no longer answers. There is blood all over the floor. I try to wipe it up, but I realize I cannot stop the flow of blood from her head. It is very quiet here. There is only the silence of death.

I start to take off her clothes. It is hard to take the clothes off a dead body. Finally it is done. Her beautiful white body is before me. I've waited so long this day and now it is here. I touch her ass. It is so very smooth. I wonder where I should bite first. I decide to bite the top of her butt. My nose is covered with her cold white skin. I try to beat down hard, but I can't. I suddenly have a horrible headache. I get a knife from the kitchen and stab it deeply into her skin. Suddenly a lot of sallow fat oozes from the wound. It reminds me of Indian corn. It continues to ooze. It is strange. Finally I find the red meat under the sallow fat. I scoop it out and put it in my mouth. I chew. It has no smell and no taste. It melts in my mouth like a perfect piece of tuna. I look in her eyes and say: You are delicious.

I cut her body and lift the meat to my mouth again and again. Then I take a photograph of her white corpse with its deep wounds. I have sex with her body. When I hug her she lets out a breath. I'm frightened, she seems alive. I kiss her and tell her I love her. Then I drag her body to the bathroom. By now I am exhausted, but I cut into her hip and put the meat in a roasting pan. After it is cooked I sit at the table using her underwear as a napkin. They still smell of her body.

Finally she is in my stomach. Finally she is in my stomach. Finally she is mine. It is the best dinner I've ever had. Afterward I sleep with her. Next morning she is still here. She doesn't smell bad

It's been twenty-four hours now. Some huge flies hover and buzz in the bathroom. I try to chase them away, but they came back. They swarm on her face. They seem to tell me that I've lost her forever. It is no longer her. Where is she? She's gone far away. I've broken her. Like a child who breaks his toy.

I try to use the electric knife, but it doesn't work very well. It just makes its shrill sound. So I use the hatchet. I imagine myself on the guillotine. It is surprisingly easy to cut through. With the head gone her body is now only flesh. When I grab the hair and hang up the head, I realize I am a cannibal.

I turn the TV and open the refrigerator. I put the dishes on the glass table. I recognize each pieces of meat. This is part of her hip and this is part of her thigh. I fry them on the stove. I set the table. There is mustard, salt, pepper and sauce. I put her underwear beside the dish. I sniff it and look at a nude woman in a magazine. I try to remember which part of her is in my mouth, but it is difficult to connect the meat with a body. It just seems like a piece of meat. I continue to eat her body until I am caught. Each day the meat becomes more tender, each day the taste is more sweet and delicious.

AFTERWORD

I've been experimenting for about a year with the notion that everything I do could be visible, transparent. That with nothing to hide and everything to show, my life would become something I could track and watch.

I was explaining this to someone recently and it struck me that for over a year I have put just about every bit of myself that I could into the internet, either visually or in writing. I can look back and note the dates of anything significant and look at all my work and see if I've made any progress.

I don't know if I have. That saddens me some. It also means I will be calling an end to this experiment. Nothing will be removed; I won't black out my page or take anything down.

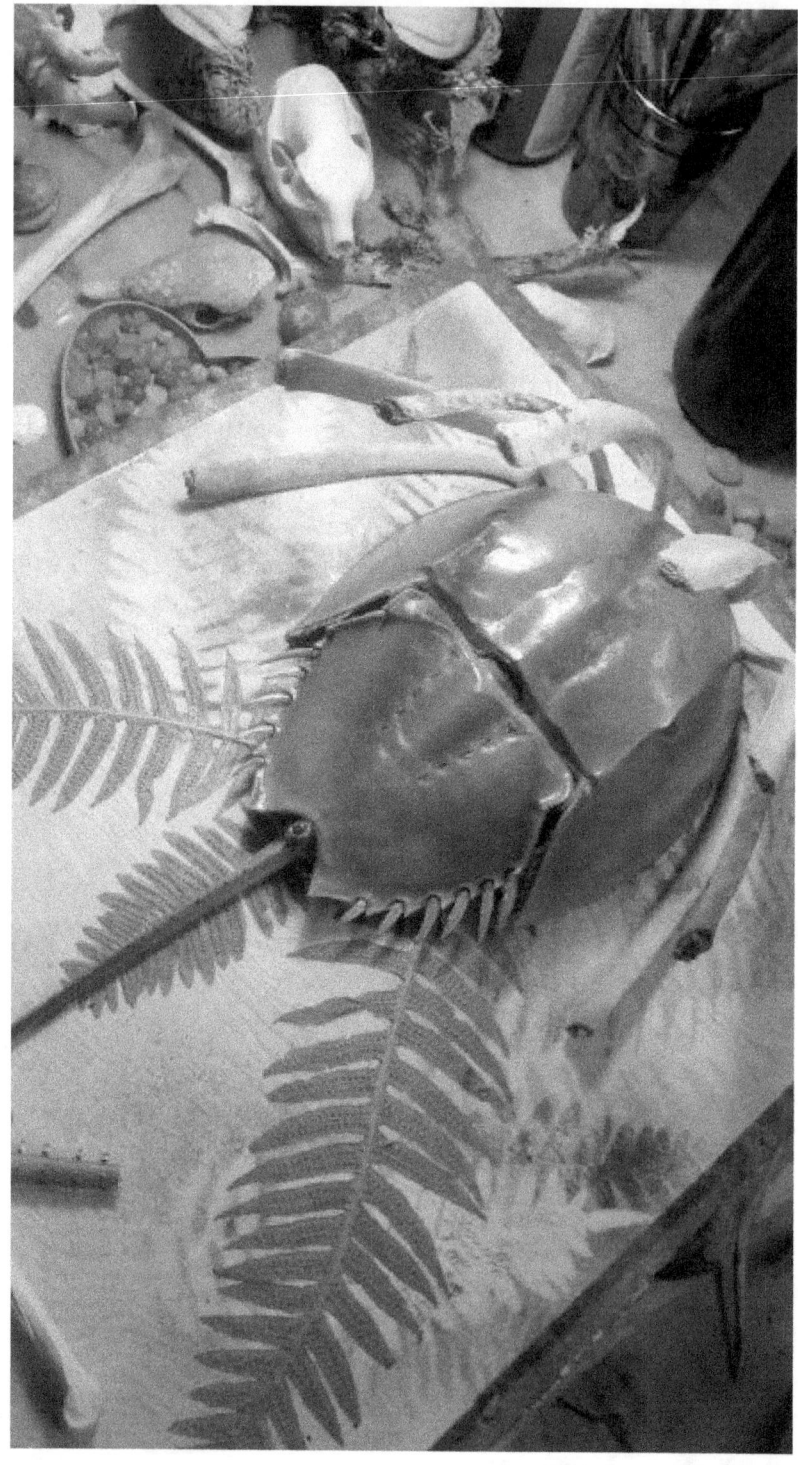

It's not any one thing that makes me think I need to pull out for a while, there's a lot of stuff that's been going on for me that I just don't think is going to be resolved for me unless I stop feeding this monster I made.

And for my own sake I have to do it.

If you've been following my work and my writing this last year or so, thank you so much for your time and attention. I think knowing you, dear reader, were there, meant a lot more to me than you might think. I'll be posting the Brag over at my website, and paintings as I do them. But the half-formed thoughts and strange rants and the sketches and unfinished things will be no more, not for a while.

FINAL NOTES

Final thoughts for people wishing to become professional tattoo artists.

As a tattoo artist for the last ten years, I've seen many people who are interested in learning the trade. I've also seen many make the mistake of trying to take a shortcut to becoming a tattoo artist at home, or as a hobby.

If you are planning to tattoo "for fun" or as a hobby, you should know that in most states this is illegal. The biggest, and most serious reason, is for the health and safety of your (potential) clients. Tattooing in a bacteria-ridden space, with unsterilized equipment, or even worse, non-disposable equipment, is extremely risky.

The risks associated with home tattooing start with minor Staph infections and end with septicemia (which can be fatal) and transmission of serious, life-threatening viruses. Also, using your home as a tattoo studio puts you and your family at extreme risk of infections and diseases. Simply put, this is not safe, and is most likely against the law.

When you decide to learn tattooing it's best to be careful. There are unscrupulous people who will try to take advantage of your interest, and knowing the usual steps taken to become a tattoo artist can help you avoid them.

Having an interest in tattooing and being able to draw, while necessary, are not the only things you'll need. You'll also require a lot of dedication, patience, and sociability. It is hard to become a tattoo artist because it weeds out those who aren't equipped with these necessities.

If you're the typical starving artist, tattooing can look very lucrative compared to where you're at right now, but it's not really a craft you can learn on your own (despite what those unscrupulous people might say).

If you can't be patient and persistent, you won't be a good tattooist anyway. Dealing with clients is much more difficult than learning to tattoo, and without the barriers and obstacles to learning there would be no way to ensure the temperament of potential tattooists.

Tattooing is a job in which you will permanently apply images to other people's bodies. You will be exposed to needle-stick hazards, infectious diseases, unconsciousness, rudeness, vomiting, blood, bad smells, and frightened folks. You'll have to know how to write "strength" in chinese, japanese, and farsi, and how to soothe a large scary biker who is crying for his mommy. You'll be busy at work for a full shift and then go home to draw for five hours to get ready for the next day.

You will have to get vaccinations, business licenses, and confidence in your drawing ability. And you'll be rewarded by working with people you love, looking how you like, and creating art that people love enough to wear forever. If you're really good, you might even become famous, work at conventions, be published in magazines, or write books.

It's a serious job and carries a lot of responsibility. It involves the trust of every person that you will tattoo-that you know how to keep them safe, and how to do the tattoo correctly.

Tattoo artists are unwilling to apprentice people who are not interested in tattooing as a career. The amount of work and time it takes to properly train someone to tattoo safely just isn't worth it. Learning on your own will not allow you the ability to use modern techniques and equipment, since most retailers will not sell professional-grade equipment to amateurs. Despite what you may have read on the internet, there are NO books that will teach you everything you need to know to be a tattoo artist. These will only give you bits of information, and without good, working equipment and true, complete information, you just can't tattoo all that well.

If you're planning on doing this for fun, don't bother. It is an actual, honest-to-god, real-life career, and should be approached as one.

If you decide that you do want to make a career of tattooing, you're halfway there. Making the commitment to learn is the same as any other skilled occupation-it will take a few years to become proficient, and it will take initiative to learn. Most tattoo artists eventually have one or more apprentices, so if you are dedicated and persistent your chances are good.

Start by making a resume. List your work experience, and your art background, if you have any. As your cover page, write a brief synopsis of the reasons you'd like to become a tattoo artist, and what it means to you. Seeing a professional resume instead of being asked verbally to teach makes a great deal of difference, and puts you ahead of the dabblers. It gives you a professional appearance, and allows the artist you want to learn from to take you seriously.

Assemble a small portfolio of drawings, photographs, and paintings you've done, and make several bound copies of it at kinko's on the color copier. If you don't draw, consider taking an art class or two before you start trying to learn tattooing. Despite events on recent television shows, it's much easier to learn one skill set at a time. You can ask a tattoo artist for guidance about which classes might apply or be useful, but a basic drawing, color theory, or figure drawing class is good even for experienced draftsmen.

Include in your book anything you really think is good, some things that aren't, and things you think are possible to make into tattoos. This will give the artist you speak with some idea of what your abilities are and what you might be capable of as a tattooist.

If they ask you to come back some other time, try to get a specific time and don't show up late. Remember that not all tattoo artists want to or have time to teach. If they blow you off at the start, think of it as a cue to try someone else as a teacher. They may be trying to soften the blow by saying they're too busy to talk to you, not trying to be rude. Ask if they know of anyone else you can speak with, since they may know someone who can help you. Becoming a tattoo artist is a process, and it may take

time to find people who will take you seriously and help you out.
You may have to move to a different city or area in order to learn. Think
of this as paying your dues. Many many people have to move to go to
the college of their choice, and never end up working in the field they
got a degree in! You can rest assured that with dedication, your
sacrifice will be worth it. If there are other priorities in your life that
prevent you from moving, and you can't find anyone close enough to
teach you, it's probably not meant for you to become a tattoo artist.
The demands of the work often interfere heavily with other priorities
and "having a life", so think twice if there are reasons you can't move.
Tattooing will interfere with them even if you end up learning locally
and you may regret the decision later.
Contacting artists on the internet is always a good idea. Write to people
whose art you admire and ask them if they take apprentices, or if they
know of anyone who does.
Getting your portfolio color-copied and bound at kinko's may cost a
few dollars, but it is a good idea because you can ask these artists for
help, advice, and criticism. Many experienced artists will accept your
book and resume and give you help with it. Asking if you can send them
something to look at and asking for criticism can help you find someone
to teach you, as most tattoo artists have a professional network of
friends. Corresponding with one person can bring your desire to learn
to the attention of many.
When soliciting criticism, try to take it well. Becoming defensive or
making excuses will only stop the other person from helping you again.
Listen to their advice and try to use as much as you can.
When you find someone who will apprentice you, for your own
protection you should get a written agreement to teach. This should be
something like a contract that lists what they will teach you, and states
what will happen to you when you're done learning(i.e. will they hire
you? for how much pay? for how long?) It should also estimate the
length of the apprenticeship to within a few months. The price of the

teaching and the amount of "gruntwork" should also be listed. This can easily be put together by sitting down together and just writing down as much of the information as you can, and both signing it.

To be a tattoo artist, you'll need OSHA training in bloodborne pathogens and cross-contamination controls, as well as CPR/first aid. You'll also need to learn a lot about dermatology and the nervous system. Learning about equipment, maintenance, and supplies is also pertinent, as is learning about the engineering of the human body.

Tattoo artists are cross-trainers; their knowledge straddles many fields. Learning from a good artist is the best way to obtain all of this, and learning one-on-one is the best way to do it.

Be very wary of "schools" that have more than one or two students for each "instructor", and be cautious about paying for any apprenticeship that lasts less than ten months. These may be state-licensed but can't possibly give you the worth of your time and money. The amount of information you'll need to work as a tattoo artist is vast, and can't be taught in a classroom or seminar, or in a few weeks.

You should try to apprentice from someone who will hire you when you are finished. The demand for brand-new tattoo artists is so low as to be negligible. Try to get a job with your instructor when you are done, at least for a year or two. Talk about this before you pay any money or invest time in learning. If they won't hire their own student, that says very little about the quality of their teaching!

Last but not least, if you are serious and determined about tattooing, if you love it more than anything, and if you are willing to spend your life with it, you WILL find a teacher. Don't give up hope! As a famous tattoo artist once said, "Tattooing is a special job for special people, it takes care of its own, and you'll always get out of it what you put into it."

ABOUT THE AUTHOR

Anji Marth is a professional tattoo artist living in the Pacific Northwest. She has lived in ten states and twice as many cities, travels often, and enjoys coffee, reading nonfiction medical history books, horror movies, rock climbing, hellraising, and deep-woods hiking.

She can be reached through her website at resonanteye.net and currently lives with her partner, and her dog, in Washington state.

www.ingramcontent.com/pod-product-compliance
Lightning Source LLC
Chambersburg PA
CBHW051213170526
45166CB00005B/1883